I'LL GET IT DONE

A Life Journey in Rappahannock

Lillian Freeman Aylor

Lillian Freeman Aylor

I'll Get it Done: A Life Journey in Rappahannock
© Lillian Freeman Aylor, 2019

First Edition 2nd printing
Published by Bair Ink www.bairink.com
Fredericksburg, VA, USA

Cover photograph and photo restorations by E. Raymond Boc
Photo page 94 by Molly Peterson
Other photos and clippings reprinted with permission

Library of Congress Control Number: 2019955212
ISBN: 978-1-7329042-8-6

I'LL GET IT DONE
A Life Journey in Rappahannock

Lillian Freeman Aylor

EMERGING AUTHORS

Fredericksburg, Virginia

"This book shows with persevering faith you can rise above the pitfalls of life, get an education and be proud of your accomplishments."

—Aline B. Johnson, Rappahannock Co School Board member 1998-2018

"Whether you are new to Rappahannock or a long-time resident, you will be amazed when you read about Lillian Aylor's life and find that she seems to be the matriarch of the County. Through family, work, and friendships she has touched almost everyone here. Delightful, nostalgic, clear-eyed and honest."

—Ann Stenner, elementary school teacher for 28 years

"This was a compelling story about growing up as a bi-racial woman in a rural county in Virginia before and during the Civil Rights movement. It was appalling to me how long racial discrimination continued to affect the daily lives of the non-white community where I now live. Lillian's strength and willingness to help others guides her though those turbulent times. This is a story that needs to be heard."

— Aleta Gadino, GMU Student Services Health counselor, Elementary School Instructional Assistant and horticulturist and co-owner of Gadino's Wine cellar.

ACKNOWLEDGMENTS

I would like to thank the many people, family and friends who helped me pull my story together. It takes a community to make a life, and Rappahannock has given me all of that, for which I feel gratitude and pride:

Tom Knisely, Jan McKinney, Brittany Dwyer, Ray Boc, Barbara Adolfi, Mary-Sherman Willis, Kim Aylor Beard, Richard Freeman, Barbara Hemmons, Bessie Grigsby, Bruce Sloane, Molly Peterson, Aline Johnson, Ann Stenner, Aleta Gadino and Cliff Miller III.

This memoir is made possible by two grants from RAAC's Claudia Mitchell Arts Funds.

Also, my thanks to the Rappahannock Historical Society for their help with the history of African-Americans in the county. And the Scrabble School Preservation Foundation for their assistance in securing funding for this project.

TABLE OF CONTENTS

TABLE OF CONTENTS continued

INTRODUCTION

My life has been a journey through time in one place, Rappahannock County. My people come from here and it's always been home, even when I left it for a while. As Robert Frost said, "Home is the place where, when you have to go there, they have to take you in." Even though many of us old timers have left the county, and many young people too, for me it's always been the place to come home to.

The county itself has been on its own journey in time. My life here is as much a story of the county as it is my story. My struggles and my joys have been the joys and struggles of my community. My one story is the story of many.

In this book, you will learn about life in Rappahannock before and after desegregation, what the black community was like, how we lived and were educated, what the challenges and pleasures were in life in the county.

You can find that story in the people, our churches, our schools, our homes and neighborhoods, our food, our music, and our history.

I never thought that I would become a writer. I was always jotting stuff down but had no idea to become a writer. And I never would have, if I had not gotten all the encouragement from our guests at the Inn at Mount Vernon Farm.

Over time, people have taken an interest in my story and interviewed me. Several years ago, I was interviewed by a teacher at Rappahannock County High School, Jan McKenney, as part of an oral history project. And then, a couple of years ago a graduate of Rappahannock High School, Brittany Dwyer, needed to do a social work paper for a class at George Mason University. She chose to write it on me. In March of 2015, Tom Knisley, a regular guest at the Inn at Mount. Vernon Farm, collected Brittany's interview and his own interview with me and compiled them, and a large collection of family photographs, into a beautiful book, *My Rappahannock Journey: The Life of Lillian Freeman Aylor.*

After our guests read the article about the food at the Inn at Mount Vernon Farm in the magazine *Edible DC*, they were telling me, "Well I hope some of your recipes are going to be in this book. We want the book." So, I've added in some of my favorite recipes from the Inn at Mount Vernon Farm kitchen.

I'll tell my own story, the story of a community and a way of life that is gone. Some good parts, some not so good. I won't be here forever, and when I'm gone, there's no one left to tell it.

Within this small county I've come a long way, and I'm still close to home.

And in the end, home is all about the cooking!

LIFE IN THE HOLLOWS

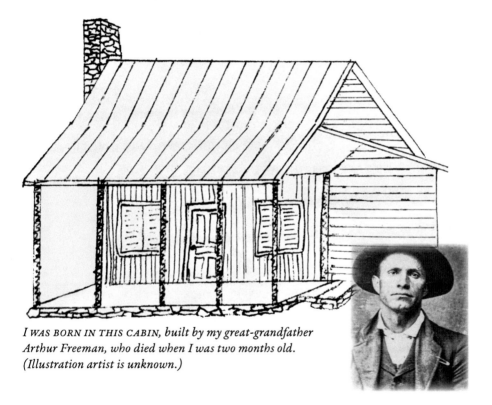

I WAS BORN IN THIS CABIN, built by my great-grandfather Arthur Freeman, who died when I was two months old. (Illustration artist is unknown.)

I grew up in Rappahannock County in a place called Gid Brown Hollow. These days the whole area is called Gid Brown Hollow. Back when I was growing up it was actually three different areas. There was Gid Brown, which was the lower area. That area was named for Gideon Brown. Another area on up the road was called Smedley Hollow and that is where I lived. The Smedley Store was down in Gid Brown Hollow. The third area was called Keyser Hollow.

Gid Brown Hollow is part of the Hampton District near Little Washington in the middle of Rappahannock County. We're very close to the Shenandoah National Park and the trails there. The main road leading to Washington, Virginia, known as Little Washington, winds through a deep valley surrounded by foothill mountains like Jenkins Mountain. We lived high up on one of those foothills.

It was mostly farms, and apple and cherry orchards, which employed the men; some of the women cleaned and cooked for the owners. Most of the African-Americans owned their own homes and the ones who didn't had houses furnished to them on the farm where they worked.

We were poor but not living in total poverty. We kids grew up in a four-room cabin at the foot of the mountain. We could not have some things we wanted, but always had food because we had gardens, we butchered hogs. We raised our own chickens and had our own eggs. We sold eggs to the Smedley Store and took the money and bought some other staples we needed.

I grew up surrounded by family and relatives. My great-uncle Wade Freeman and his family lived just down the hill from us; that is where we got our milk every day. Uncle Wade's daughter, Mildred Freeman, was so sweet to me. I would go to their house with my mother or grandmother, whichever I went with, and didn't want to leave. So, Mildred would take me back up the hill. She couldn't wait for me to come down to see my uncles. The whole family, Uncle Wade and everybody, they took to me. I was the youngest kid around, so they just adored me and walked me up and down the hill.

Mildred lived to be 98 years old and had a great memory up until her death in 2018. She would talk about those walks until her last days. I used to ask her about things I couldn't remember! Even when I visited her in the nursing home, she let it be known I was "her girl."

My cousin Mildred wrote poetry about our Rappahannock life. You can find some of those poems in Appendix I.

Our neighborhood was a sharing place. If you happen to be out of sugar, flour, or meal, you would go and borrow it and pay it back when you went to the store.

Once in a while we would go to the Fletcher's Mill in Sperryville to get cornmeal and flour for ourselves, and feed for the hogs. There was once a mill in Gid Brown Hollow, but it had ceased to operate when I was old enough to know about it. Once in a while we would walk to the Sperryville Corner Store, which then was Schwartz's Store, where they sold shoes, clothing, food and pretty much what you needed for your home. Also, the Lea Brothers Store in Washington sold pretty much what you could get in Sperryville.

I remember when I was just a little more than three years old, my great-aunt Eva Summons went to leave the store and saw this beautiful little red snowsuit, and she got it for me. I just loved that little snowsuit.

Growing up in Gid Brown Hollow before I was a teen was not too bad. At that time there were a lot of children. We played together, had fun birthday parties at one house or another. But it was not all play. We had chores to do also, such as pulling weeds in the garden in the springtime and feeding them to the pigs, or gathering eggs, which I loved to do. Usually hogs were killed around Thanksgiving time and I could not wait until the meat was cut up so I could grind it for sausage. Also stirring lard in an iron kettle over an open fire outside was fun for me.

In the fall we made apple butter. I just love homemade apple butter made outside. We set up a big copper kettle in the yards of people's houses, and several families would get together from the hollow. Someone has to stir it all the time for twelve hours and keep a fire going under the kettle. It takes a day to peel and cut up all the apples, and the next day to stir. I've been making apple butter all my life. Usually, I'm the last one who gets it in the jars sterilized in boiling water. That's the fun part. I love the finished product. In the last few years that I made it, we cooked it at the Mount Vernon Farm Dairy Barn and I sold it at the store. Friends of my boss Cliff Miller could buy it by the case. My blackberry jam is popular too although I didn't get any made in 2019, as bears, wild geese, and wild birds ate up all the berries before I could get to them.

CHURCH LIFE IN THE OLD DAYS

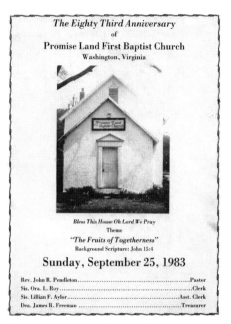

The Eighty Third Anniversary
of
Promise Land First Baptist Church
Washington, Virginia

Bless This House Oh Lord We Pray
Theme
"The Fruits of Togetherness"
Background Scripture: John 15:4

Sunday, September 25, 1983

Rev. John R. Pendleton..............................Pastor
Sis. Ora. L. Roy......................................Clerk
Sis. Lillian F. Aylor............................Asst. Clerk
Dea. James R. Freeman..........................Treasurer

We all loved going to church. We would all walk to The Promised Land Baptist Church up in Gid Brown Hollow. There were a lot of black people in the area at that time. At that time, we also had Sunday evening services. We all loved walking back from church in the evening.

The Pastor's sermons were about The Work of giving our lives to Jesus, of being a good and active Christian, to do things for people and get along with them. These were lessons I heard all through my childhood attending Sunday School, from the time I was a little girl into adulthood. I've been a devoted churchgoer all my life. Ultimately, I became the superintendent of Sunday School for the Promised Land Church, and spread the message of living a life devoted to God. Those early sermons set the foundation for me being who I am now.

Almost always the Pastor would go to one of the parishioners' home for dinner. When they would leave, the person would always pack up food for the Pastor to take. We shared what we had with the Pastor. I have gone back to the minute books from the 1950's. There was very little collected. There just wasn't that much money coming in, that's why pastors were paid in food that was grown in the gardens.

Special events were held mostly at church. Birthdays for children were community affairs. All the children would come together and play games and have cake and ice cream at the birthday child's home. There were no presents exchanged but just a lot of fun.

I always loved to sing, even as a little girl. We only had one choir in church when I was a kid. One of my neighbors had a little keyboard and would go into the hymnbook and pick out a song. She would play the song and we would sing.

At 11 years old, I was baptized and started singing with the church choir and attended Sunday School. Some 68 years later I am the only choir member still singing in the choir at Promised Land Baptist Church, and the only woman. We have some men that joined back in the 70's and 80's.

In 1995 I started taking piano lessons with Leslie Nichols until she got married and moved to Stafford, VA. Here's a coincidence. When I was in elementary school, we had a visiting music teacher by the name of Miss Charlotte Golladay from the Harrisonburg area. Miss Golladay became the wife of Mr. Paul Nichols, and their daughter was Leslie, my piano teacher. Also Mrs. Charlotte Nichols accompanied me at funerals at the Episcopal Church in Little Washington when I was singing. After her daughter Leslie moved a few years later, I continued to have lessons at Rappahannock High School with a teacher from Shenandoah University. These were lessons that Kathryn Treanor set up at the high school. I did a year with her and then she was called full-time at the university. But she had three students over here and drove over to each of us and gave lessons at our houses. I really loved her.

***

I sure remember holidays as good times. I remember at Christmas time all the older members of the family would come home. A lot of them had moved away because there weren't any jobs for them to do here in this area. Most of the time they would come home for a couple of weeks. A lot of the men folks that didn't have children left Rappahannock for employment in some other state and came home for two weeks for Christmas and New Year.

Christmas morning, we got up early to see what Santa had brought. What we got under the tree was nuts, candy and oranges and maybe a pair of socks, stockings or gloves. Back then we didn't get things all the time, like kids do now. It was just that one time a year. But we were as happy as if we had gotten a hundred dollars. After opening the gifts, we ate breakfast, and the rest of the day we went from house to house eating and seeing what others got for Christmas.

I remember waiting for Christmas to come. It seemed like it would never get here. I knew when everyone came home we were going to have a good time. It was wonderful.

I think that's why kids aren't as grateful now. They get things the whole year round. Now when Christmas comes, it doesn't make any difference to them. It seems like nothing whatsoever. I remember we looked forward to the Christmas church service and also the Christmas play. I keep thinking, why can't those times be now? I sure miss those times in Gid Brown Hollow. It was just a loving community. If there was death in one house everybody came together. Everyone brought food in to them; they didn't have to cook. I miss all of that.

Every August there would be Homecoming. The church would fill up with family members from Philadelphia, New York, Maryland, everywhere. Each family would fix a whole dinner by themselves. Then starting at three in the morning, they'd get ready to have the food to bring to church. They set up permanent tables outside and they'd get filled with food. You've never seen so much food in your life! We had fried chicken, ham, sweet potatoes and beans, macaroni, potato salad, corn pudding, cakes and pies and drinks. My grandmother made Tyler pudding pie, a custardy pie that's made with vinegar, and I loved it! Sometime my grandfather Mundy brought some of his mutton (I hated it!). Now Homecoming is on the fourth Sunday in September each year. That's because we had a lot of old-school Church people from Harris Hollow who came to our church. Their Association met in August, and so we moved our Homecoming to accommodate them and we could go there.

MY FAMILY

I was born at home on October 23, 1938. A midwife named Lizzie Hughes helped out. She delivered practically every one of us up there. I was born at five in the morning while everyone was sleeping. There was no phone, so my grandmother walked about a quarter mile down the hill to get the midwife. I was my mother's first baby.

There's actually a contradiction on my birth date. After I lost my birth certificate, I drove down to Richmond to get a new one. It said I was born the 21st! They explained that they didn't get the information until two days after I was born. So, the 21st is the official date. So, I get two birthdays!

There were ten people in our household: my grandmother, mother, two male cousins, three brothers, two sisters and myself. My mother raised us without our father. She had six children: me, the oldest, then James, Forrest, with our father Richard Freeman. Then came Anna and the twins, Arlene and Darlene, that my mother had with Raymond Poles, who was related to my father. His mother and my father's mother were sisters. (In my family, it stays in the family!) Like my father, Raymond didn't live with us; he eventually moved to Philadelphia.

After my youngest brother Forrest was born, my dad left Rappahannock County to go to Plainfield, NJ. He told my mom he

ELIZA FREEMAN VENEY,
My paternal great grandmother.

JANE OLDEN,
My paternal grandmother.

JAMES ROBERT MUNDY,
My grandfather.

ROSIE FREEMAN,
My grandmother.

ROBERT MUNDY JR.
My uncle (mother's half brother).

My father, Richard Robinson Freeman.

My mother, Bertha Freeman. About 1952.

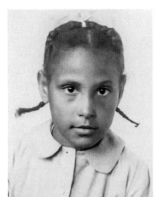

Lillian Freeman

My brother, James Freeman.

My brother, Forrest Freeman.

My sisters and brothers, William, Richard, and Barbara Freeman.

My sister, Anna Freeman.

Darlene Freeman

Arlene Freeman

was going to get a job and would be back. That never happened. He stayed in Plainfield for a long time. Then up in New Jersey he married a lady from North Carolina, and they had three children. So, my mom was a single parent.

It was very embarrassing for me, especially in the first couple of grades. Other children's parents would come to school to things, but only my mother and grandmother came with me. Kids started asking me where my father was. And at that time, I always answered, "I don't have a father." When I got older, I told them, "My mother's not married."

My father's side of the family, the Freemans, was almost all white. My mother's side was more mixed.

We lived with my Grandma Rosie, my mother's mother. My mother worked a lot, usually for the D. Lyle Miller family. When she was working, Grandma was at home taking care of us. When Forrest was born, my mother stayed home, and my grandma went to work. Grandma worked for the Snead family, who were also white. I would walk over to the Sneads with my Grandma. Miss Marjorie, their daughter, would take me back and forth to Charlottesville where she was a nurse at the University of Virginia Hospital. My great uncles also worked for the Sneads. A lot of our family worked for them.

My father worked as a truck driver for Mr. and Mrs. John Snead Sr. taking their apples to Winchester. Their son, John P. Snead Jr, was a doctor. He was our physician here in Sperryville. She would take me to UVA for my doctor's appointments. We also had a neighbor, Esther Racer. She would take me also. Dr. John P. Snead was everyone's doctor. If someone was sick, he did house calls. My grandmother Rosie told me that Dr. Snead came to see my great-grandfather Arthur Freeman when he was suffering, most likely of heart disease. Dr. Snead referred to him as Uncle Arthur and would say how much he wished he could make him well and take him out of his discomfort. Both my grandmother Rosie and my great-grandfather worked for Dr. Snead for a long time.

We all always had a good relationship with the Snead family. A few years ago, a lady stayed here at the Inn at Mount Vernon Farm. Her name was Caroline and her mother was a Snead, who were people I knew. They wanted to know about me, and I wanted to know about them. She called her mother Betty in Florida, and told her where she was, and had seen me. A couple of years ago, Dr. John Payton Snead III, the son of our family doctor, and his wife Sharon spent the night at the Inn and they were so happy to see me

***

I want to say how important my grandmother Rosie was in my life. She was from the Blackfoot Tribe and was part Indian. You could tell from her features she was part Native American. She was a person who was so peaceful and quiet. I never saw her really angry. But yet we knew not to do anything wrong around her, even though we had never seen her angry. I just admired her so much; she was such a sweet person. Everyone around loved her. My cousins felt the same.

A few years before my cousin Raymond Freeman passed, I would take him back and forth to the doctor's and the Veteran's Hospital in Martinsburg, West Virginia. He would say, "You are so much like your grandmother." That felt so comforting. My other cousin, Major Freeman said, "Lillian, you're so much like your Grandmother." I felt like that was a great accomplishment because she was such a lovely person.

23

***

My father's family, the Freemans, worked for the Millers, who were white farmers in Rappahannock. They had two farms in the county. When I was growing up my mother did not talk about who my grandfather was, but many years later, when I was about 40 years old, my Aunt Margaret told me I that Mr. Brooke Robert Miller Sr. was my great-grandfather, and that his son Brooke Menefee Miller was my grandfather. That would mean that my grandfather was white. It didn't bother me too much, growing up. I just never talked about it. It would be years before I found out the truth about that.

By the time I was born, my great aunt Eliza Freeman Evans was the cook at the Brooke Miller farm in Gid Brown Hollow. Every time I would go over to see my great aunt—I was just a little bitty girl—Mr. Miller Sr. would always be sitting on the porch up there and see us coming over. He called me "Little Boy" (I don't know why!) and he would say, "Little Boy, I'll give you a dime to go back over there and get the mail." So, I always loved to go, because he always gave me a dime. That dime would buy a whole lot of candy or cookies! I could get a whole bag full. So, I couldn't wait to go over there to visit my great-aunt.

My mother also worked for Mr. and Mrs. D. Lyle Miller, Sr., for years until they passed. He was the brother of Brooke Robert Miller, Sr. Then she worked for their son, D. Lyle Miller, Jr., and his wife Louise Miller, who was a teacher from Orange, VA. My mother worked for them for years and years until she had the twins.

Mrs. Louise Miller was so nice to my mother; she even took her to the hospital when the twins were born. She would also take them back and forth to see the doctor. At that time, I had to help my mother take care of the twins, so I felt like I was a mother when I was fourteen. Taking care of the kids well prepared me to be a mom. I also worked in the orchard to have enough money to go to high school. I needed the money to pay for my books and other things.

***

My dad, Richard Robinson Freeman, would come down from New Jersey and see us about once a year, when he visited his aunt Eva Summons, his mother's sister. It was always in the summertime, probably his vacation time. I got to spend a little time with him at Aunt Eva's house. Mostly it was the three of us children who went, James, Forrest and myself, since we were old enough to go by ourselves. We'd eat sandwiches and catch up. Sometimes his mother, my Grandma Jane (Cora Jane Freeman Olden), would come down too from New Jersey to visit. She had moved up there years earlier.

Aunt Eva was an important link for us to my father. Even years later, when my father was retiring and needed his social security, he found he didn't have his birth certificate. When he was born, all births and deaths in the black community went down in the family Bible or the cookbook. Dad wrote to me about his certificate, and I went to Aunt Eva to see what she had. We found his name and birth date in her old cookbook. We took the book to Judge Rayner Snead, who accepted it as evidence of my father's birth, and so we were able to get him a birth certificate, and then his Social Security.

My great-aunt, Aunt Georgia Porter, was really my idol. Even so, I thought she was the meanest woman I ever knew. She used to say, "If you don't behave yourself, you will get into trouble and I will send you to reform school." She would scare me. I think she knew I wasn't going to do anything anyway, but she would always tell me that.

She and Uncle Will had an old one-seater car. They were raising their grandson, William Porter Jr. (we grew up together and we graduated together too) and they would take me to church with them. We would ride in the back of the car; sometimes we would ride up in the windshield part. People would laugh when we got to church, but we didn't care that we were riding.

We would sometimes walk to the store and go by their house on the way, and we would be really quiet passing, because we knew Aunt Georgia would have us come in for some reason. Somehow, she always knew when we were on that road! She would come out and call us in to visit and give us something to eat. And, of course, tell me I was going to be sent to reform school if I wasn't good.

When she was older, she had her leg amputated. She lived in Little Washington with her sister and brother, Virgie and McCoy Williams. I would go and visit, and by then I thought she was the sweetest person I ever knew. One day I said to her, "You know what, I'm glad you told me I better not do anything bad." I knew if I did something bad, I would be punished. That is a good thing to know.

My great-grandfather on my mother's side, Arthur Freeman, and my great-grandmother on my father's side, Eliza Freeman Veney, were brother and sister. Since I have been a member of the Rappahannock Historical Society, I found out that some black members of my family fought in the Civil War, probably for the Union. A former student from the George Washington Carver School did research and presented it at the Scrabble School Preservation Foundation, and I found a lot of ancestors and neighbors I knew had been in the Civil War, especially some Veneys. After the War they stayed here in Gid Brown Hollow in Rappahannock County.

LIVING WITH SEGREGATION

My first couple of years in school I was very sickly; I had a sore throat all winter. When I was about nine years old, they decided to have my tonsils taken out. It was done at UVA Medical Center in Charlottesville. My mother went with me. That was the first time that I knew that things were different for white and black people. At the hospital, one side of the waiting room said WHITE and the other side said COLORED. The bathrooms were the same.

In the hospital, the wards were segregated. The colored had one section and the whites had another section.

I didn't think much about it. We were separated anyway, at school, for instance.

Before segregation was formally abolished in 1970, we couldn't go everywhere we wanted in Rappahannock. For instance, there was a restaurant in Amissville, the Bellaire, where we had to go in by the back door to get food to carry out. It was where the Mayhugh Store is now. Growing up in Gid Brown Hollow, as a kid, we had very few privileges.

If we went to the movies at the Theatre in Little Washington, we had to go up and sit in the balcony. There used to be a bus that ran from Luray to Front Royal that we rode to go shopping, or just to visit relatives and friends. If you were black, you had to go to the back. The spring where we got our water was about 100 feet down the road from our house. We would make sure that we would not be on the road when the bus came along because the white children on there would spit at us, throw things at us and call us names.

The black churches were the only places we really had to go to that were ours. That was how the Rappahannock Countywide Citizens League happened. Their large white building on Fodderstack Road in Little Washington was built in the 1940s. Members of the county black churches and parents from the four Rosenwald Schools chipped in. (I'll talk about those schools later.) The League provided a place for African-Americans to gather together safely. After desegregation, support for the League dropped off as African-Americans moved out of the county and older members died off. For years, the Inn at Little Washington rented the building for storage. The old building just went for sale and the money will be divided between eight churches.

Segregated spaces felt sort of normal since that is what we had to do. That's the way it was! I sort of blocked it out of my mind. I knew I was able to go certain places and not others. It didn't upset me. I didn't have to force myself to do something or antagonize people. In my twenties the county was still segregated. Both big schoolhouses in Rappahannock, the one in Sperryville and the one in Little Washington, were for whites only. There was no high school for blacks in Rappahannock. When I reached 8th grade, I had to take a bus to Culpeper to go to high school.

There were members of the Ku Klux Klan in the county, but I don't know too much other than what the old folks used to talk about. I heard that a lynching happened over in Huntly. And then here in Rappahannock I know of several men who had to leave the county because they had kids, got a white woman pregnant or something. They had to leave or else they would have been lynched. They had to run away. And I know one of the people, a good friend of mine that lives down in Madison now, her mother gave her up and a black family down in Castleton raised her.

I knew some members of the KKK. Most of them that I knew are now dead. There are still some Confederate flags flying in Rappahannock, which never bothered me too much until a couple of years ago, when cars and pickups started driving through the county flying the flags. Now that it's come back so prominently, it does bother me, especially after the white nationalist rally happened in Charlottesville in 2017. One Sunday a parade of cars with Confederate flags drove through Flint Hill and Sperryville, about 20 or so like a caravan. It makes me worry that things are starting up all over again the way they used to be.

In the old days, when a white man impregnated a black woman, that was different. They could do what they wanted and get away with it. That's what happened in my family.

My mother didn't talk about it. It was dangerous to talk about it. I gathered some of my information from the older relatives. Then later in her life, my aunt Margaret talked to me about it. She was still very bitter, even at the end of her life when her mind was slipping with Alzheimer's. Even then she was quite sure that Jack Miller was her father, that Jack had taken advantage of Grandma Rosie at some point. I don't know when because they never talked about it. He used to have wheat fields, so there was lots of work at his farm when it came time to thresh the wheat. She told me she would sometimes meet him in the road, and he would pass on by like he didn't see her. She carried that bitterness to her grave. No one ever confronted these men about the children they fathered. My mother and my grandmother, they didn't do too much talking about anything like that.

My dad's mother Jane Freeman left here and moved to New Jersey at an early age. I do know that my dad and his brother Lawrence had different fathers. Lawrence's father was a white man, but I never knew who he was.

MY FATHER, *Richard Freeman and his brother Lawrence Freeman*

SCHOOL DAYS

Until desegregation officially started in the public schools, in Rappahannock in 1966, black children received an education through 7th grade in the county, while white children were able to continue through the 12th grade.

No one in my household had schooling beyond the sixth and seventh grades because there were no high schools in Rappahannock County for African-Americans. Anyone who did get to go to high school went to the Manassas Industrial Institute, a boarding school all the way in Manassas, where their parents had to pay for their room and board. Also, in 1937 Mrs. Anna Williams Green had influenced the Rappahannock County School Board to subsidize the George Washington Carver Regional High School for the black children. It was located in Rapidan, in Culpeper County and opened in 1948, with bus transportation from four counties: Culpeper, Madison, Orange and Rappahannock.

There were originally little one-room schoolhouses for black kids in every village, like the Smedley School, which my mother went to up in Gid Brown Hollow, and the Big Branch School in Little Washington. It was located on Oven Top Road, then moved to Charlie C. Lewis's property in Sperryville on Woodward Road. There was another school in Peola Mills.

In the 1920s these small African-American schools were consolidated into four Rosenwald Graded Schools. The bigger schools could accommodate more students. There were two-room schools in Amissville, Little Washington and Scrabble. Flint Hill had a one-room school, with grades one through five, and sixth and seventh grades at the Washington Graded School, where I went to school.

Education in my family was pretty important. They wanted me to get an education because no one else had the opportunity to acquire one. My mother was a single parent when I started school, so she and my grandmother took turns going out doing housework and cooking. They also took washing and ironing in our home. In the summertime we picked wild strawberries and blackberries and sold them to get some things we needed for school. I was one month short of being seven years old when I started school in 1945 at Washington Graded. In fact, when I started school, I was already seven because school started in September and my birthday was in October. So, I was a little late starting school.

Back in the Gid Brown Hollow where we lived, there weren't too many of the black folks who had their own transportation. If the bus was running, I was able to go to school. At that age, I walked a little more than a quarter mile to catch the bus to go to school. After I got my tonsils out, we found out my eyes were bad, so I was prescribed glasses. After that I was able not to miss school anymore.

If you were black in Rappahannock and wanted to go to high school, you were bussed all the way to Culpeper County. For me that meant five years of being bussed. That was very unfair. Rappahannock had a high school right here and we had to take the bus all the way to Culpeper.

MAY DAY program at George Washington Carver High school in 1957. I was in the Queen's Court.

I attended and graduated from George Washington Carver Regional High School in Rapidan, Culpeper County, VA in the year of 1957. As the only African-American high school in the area, black students came from Orange, Madison, Culpeper and Rappahannock counties. The one bus in Rappahannock also picked up the elementary school children in Sperryville and Slate Mills, dropped them off at Scrabble School and proceeded on to the high school in Culpeper. It was a long bus ride.

Bussing those long distances to the Carver School was hard for some kids. My brother James Freeman never got used to being bussed to Carver. He would be sick every day from riding the bus that far. He just couldn't take it any longer and he quit after the ninth grade, from the stress of bussing. James never did graduate from high school. Instead, he did carpenter work with our brother Forrest, who was a bricklayer. They built homes together. Along with the church members, they built Promised Land Baptist Church in Gid Brown Hollow.

For six weeks in the fall of the first two years of high school, I worked at D. Lyle Miller's orchard, picking, grading and packing apples. They had a big packing house. This orchard was walking distance from my home in Gid Brown Hollow. A lot of people were employed there during apple picking season. The main group of employees was white folks and African-Americans from the hollow, and they were joined by black workers from Culpeper. Everyone got along well. There were no problems. When I went back to school, some of my classmates couldn't figure how I could miss six weeks and still make the honor roll. There was some jealousy and some of the students thought I was the teacher's pet, which I was not! They could not understand. I told them, "I have to work to help pay my way through school."

It just meant I had to work harder at school. That's all. I was very good at science and biology. In my senior year I was pulled from class a couple of times to teach science as a substitute because the teacher could not make it to class. It was a little frightening for me at first but then I got used to it. I was paid $35 a day to buy lunch and supplies, and I wished I had more of those days. I taught different grade levels and I had no behavior problems from the students. I knew the students. By then, everyone knew they could count on me to get something done, even though I was always called "The Quiet One." That was even remarked upon at my high school graduation.

In my senior year in high school, my English teacher asked me if I would like to participate in a competition between George Washington Carver High School and Culpeper High School. They asked that we submit a paper written about Jamestown, Virginia. My English teacher said to me, "You would be good at that subject." She asked me to submit a paper for the contest, which I did. All the teachers at Carver commented that it was superb. I turned it in and didn't even receive an Honorable Mention. Everyone was really upset. All of the judges were white. This was not fair. Only two students had entered the contest. It was well enough written to at least have gotten an honorable mention!

One weekend when I was 11th grade, my first cousin, Bessie Grisgby, and I went up to Plainfield NJ to visit my father's family. All my first cousins (Bessie, Larry, Milton, Robert and Dudley) all had gone to Plainfield to live with our grandmother. They went to school in New Jersey, and of course their schooling was completely different than here in Virginia. New Jersey schools were already integrated. They never had been segregated. Blacks and whites all went to school together. Bessie had just graduated from high school in New Jersey.

It felt really, really different. My cousin had told me about it being integrated, but I didn't really picture it that way. Once I got there, I understood the environment.

I came home from New Jersey just before my own high school graduation. My Dad gave me a suitcase for my graduation and my stepmother Estelle took me shopping and bought me my prom dress. I was treated really, really well whenever I went to Plainfield. I really adored my stepmother. She was like a mother too!

After integration the George Washington Carver Regional High School became the Piedmont Vocational High School. (Dr. Carter's name was restored in August 1993). Students attended it from four different counties. In the 1980s some of the alumni went to Richmond to have the original sign put back up as "George Washington Carver." We just didn't think it was fair that they would change the name after what created its existence. We wanted the name put back. Parents from the four counties had worked hard and did what they could to support it, my mother included. They would have dinners and other fundraisers to raise money for that school so that we could have some the most basic necessities. Many of them had not been given our opportunities. Their work for the school showed that our education was that important to them.

Several of my teachers became mentors to me and changed my life. When I was going to grade school in the seventh grade, there was a new teacher. Her name was Mrs. Julia Boddie. She had taught in Richmond and then moved to Rappahannock. And she became my idol. She taught me so much.

Mrs. Boddie would help us put on plays and I learned to sew by making costumes for the other kids at school. We made white robes for baptisms. So, I learned to do some cooking at school and some sewing. A friend of mine who is still here in the county, Marie Davis, and I did something together. There were kids who would come to school who had not had breakfast. Marie and I would take some of the powdered eggs and other items we received from the state and made breakfast for the kids. Mrs. Julia Boddie would send the two of us to the store to get other food items. She made us responsible.

Mrs. Julia Boddie knew what was in me and pulled it out. I was very shy and bashful as a child. I didn't want to do or talk about anything in front of people. She would have these plays at the First Baptist Church in Little Washington and have me perform. I'll never forget one night she had me walking down the aisle singing "Nobody Knows the Trouble I've Seen". I got through that, and another time when I had to do a recitation. I got halfway through and my mind went blank. She told me, "You're going to stand right here until you finish the piece. I know you can do it." Boy, you talk about being embarrassed; but I would have been more embarrassed if I would have sat down. Fortunately, it came to me and I finished.

When I think about all those things, I really appreciate her. That's why in 1986 I had a dream that I should honor her and give an appreciation service for her. So, I did. I called on some of her old students to help. The Lord even gave me the names of the people to ask. We formed a committee. A preacher, Reverend Howard Frye, was on the committee. He had gone to the Scrabble School, but his wife went to Washington Graded School. So, I got my committee together and put together as many names of students that Mrs. Boddie had taught and sent letters to them. A lot of people came and had a nice appreciation ceremony for her.

Then at Mrs. Dorothy Butler's suggestion, we started the Julia E. Boddie Scholarship for Rappahannock High School graduates going on to college. We gave our first scholarship in 1988 and we have been giving them ever since. We give two $500 scholarships to two students each year. Recently we gave out four scholarships, two to white students and two to the two African-American graduates of Rappahannock High. In years when we have had no black graduates, it really hurts. Often, they don't apply for the scholarships. I think it is because they are not going on in school. It's really sad. People have asked me why there aren't more blacks in Rappahannock involved in this.

My reply is, "Where are they?" Go out and look in the schools and see how many you find. But the young people, as soon as they graduate, leave because there is little work for them here.

***

Another among my idols was Mrs. Anna Green. She raised the level of education for blacks in Rappahannock and made it possible for me to further my own education past the level of my family's. Mrs. Green was a teacher in the Rosenwald School system. I took part in a panel discussion about her presented on June 17, 2015, at a conference in Durham NC to celebrate the history of the Rosenwald Schools. Here are my notes from that discussion, which gives you some history of the Rosenwald school system for black students in Virginia:

"In 1907 Anna Jeanes, a Quaker, pledged one million dollars to the betterment of basic education for blacks in rural American schools. The Jeanes Fund was unique in several respects: It was created by a woman, had a racially integrated board, became international, and existed until 1968. In Rappahannock County, the Jeanes teacher was Mrs. Anna Williams Green. She was born in 1890 in Mt. Salem, a small community just east of Washington, Virginia. She went to Philadelphia PA where she worked as a maid while living with relatives, because secondary schools for blacks were not provided in Rappahannock County. The higher wages in Philadelphia permitted her to save for education. Mrs. Green became both a model teacher of elementary courses and a highly talented and practical instructor in manual labor, teaching carpentry, sewing, tailoring, pottery, furniture repairing, cooking and other skills.

"She was appointed Supervisor of Industrial arts for the entire Rappahannock County on a regular basis between 1926 and 1943. This position was funded primarily by the Anna T. Jeanes Fund. She was also the County Supervisor for Black Schools, serving as advisor to the Superintendent and the Board of Education on black affairs, and she organized Parent-Teacher leagues throughout the County. The Parent Teacher League in Washington, Virginia purchased a 2-acre lot on Piedmont Avenue, then with the assistance of the Julius Rosenwald Fund, erected a two-room school in 1924.

"In 1937 she influenced the Rappahannock County School Board to subsidize a high school education for blacks at the Manassas Industrial Institute. Although each county paid a portion of the costs, only a limited number of black families could afford the fees for room and board, so in 1946 Mrs. Green was influential in planning for George Washington Carver Regional High School in Culpeper, a cooperative effort of Rappahannock, Orange, Madison and Culpeper Counties. It opened in 1948 with bus transportation from the four counties."

I was in her 4th grade class when she died in August 1949.

INTEGRATION COMES TO VIRGINIA

School segregation ended in Virginia in 1956. Big changes were on the way, but it took a long while, into the 1970s, for the public schools to finally desegregate. White Virginians fought the change and started a policy of Massive Resistance to make state laws to prevent integration.

Before integration, the schools for black children were pretty poor. One of the first things they did in 1966 after integration came was to install bathrooms with running water. Prior to integration the schools had outhouses. There were a few other things that also changed. They replaced the old coal stoves. The Little Washington elementary, a Rosenwald school, had a bigger playground than any of the other schools, with a baseball field. The May Day programs were held in Little Washington, when the kids from the black elementary schools in the county came together for a festival.

Lately I've been remembering what we went through and the differences between the black and the white schools. I didn't realize until I was in the 7th grade that our textbooks were different. I had a math problem and I asked my cousin Raymond, who lived with us, if he would help me. He was really good in math. Anytime I had a question, he would help.

On one occasion Raymond was helping me and he just couldn't get it done. I said don't worry, I will ask Esther Pullen. The Pullens, our next-door neighbors, were white. We often stayed at each other's houses. My brother Forrest went hiking with Bill Pullen and they stayed friends. I was friends with his sister Esther, who was also in the 7th grade. So I went over and she didn't know anything about the problem. She showed me her textbook and it was completely different. It was then that I realized we were not studying from the same books! Esther sure didn't know anything about my book. In seventh grade I found a lot out about being black.

In high school they told me that our books were passed down to us from the white schools. In New Jersey, where I visited my father, black and white students all had the same books. There wasn't any difference between the schools.

When integration first came to the Rappahannock High School, the black students were treated awfully. By that time, my younger siblings and my own children were in the system. They weren't treated badly by the teachers; it was by the other students.

Marilyn Porter, Patricia Baily, Arlene Starks and Ernestine Thompson were the first black students to go to the integrated Rappahannock High School and they had a rough time. Kids would knock them up against the walls as they walked down the hall. They had us go to the bathroom to eat lunch because the black kids weren't allowed to eat lunch in the cafeteria. Patricia cried every day, she was treated so meanly by the students.

My brother-in-law Paul Aylor also went there. He was in one of the first classes of black students who went there. He tried to ignore to the issue. It was scary for those students in the beginning. The trip between home and where we had to go to High School was quite a distance. You just had to get used to the treatment after it was happening every day.

At that time, I knew a lot of people were fighting for integration. There was a family in Front Royal that was pushing to get the black kids into the schools. Someone killed a calf and put it in their front yard. There were all kinds of mean things being done to that family. It made it a little scary. They closed the high school in Front Royal because black students were supposed to attend there. Integration did not come easy or peacefully.

They still continued bussing black children to far-away schools. Charlie Lewis, who lived in Sperryville, started a petition for our kids to be able to go to the school that was nearest to them. I signed it. My son Pete had been going to Washington Graded School and I had to take him all the way over there and back every day, when there was a school right near us in Sperryville. So, after the petition was accepted, when school opened up again, Pete started fourth grade at the Sperryville School, which had been an all-white school. Now he could be in a school closer to home. It felt different to be able to claim our rights and get a result! I became an activist for equal rights!

I was encouraged when John F. Kennedy became president. I thought he would be a good president and make a difference. I remember when Kennedy was assassinated. I was working for a family just outside of Little Washington in Tiger Valley, the Oscar Lindgrens. They were a Swedish family. They had a party that evening but when the news came, everyone's eyes were glued to the television all night.

When Martin Luther King came to the forefront, I was really happy. I was glad to know there was someone that had the nerve to stand up for equal rights. Even in the middle of the riots and everything else that was going on, he stood, he stood. It was a great thing for us. It made me happy that there was someone, no matter what, who would go through this world fighting for equal rights. The kids didn't talk about it, but we parents were really happy for him in coming forth. It was the same way with Rosa Parks. She was a very courageous woman.

So that was a sad, sad day when Dr. King was assassinated. The person who had done so much for us was gone. I just didn't believe it happened. It crossed my mind that everything was going to go back to the way it was before. I wondered if anyone was going to pick up with what he was doing.

To my knowledge white people never said anything. However, I am sure there were white people here who wanted equal rights for everyone. They just didn't or couldn't say anything. There was a lot of peer pressure here and that was the same up North. For a while it put a strain on us. When my brother Forrest went to see his white friend Bill Pullen in the Winchester hospital, they were not going to let him in. But Forrest told the people that he was a preacher (which he is) and he was given permission to go into the room. Later Bill Pullen and Manley Bruce both came to visit Forrest in the Inova Hospital when he was injured by a tractor rolling over on him. So, it's possible to be close friends and stay friends for a lifetime, regardless of skin color.

During the riots after the assassination, everything was quiet here, although it was different. You had to be here to experience the environment. We were integrated, but with the older white people in this county it was still segregated in some of their minds. Most of the people during that time got along fine. No one ever said anything to me; it was just a little different with the older white people.

You sometimes had to choose not to get involved to keep things peaceful.

My daughter Janice's experience was different from Pete's. She started first grade at the Scrabble School in the year 1967-68. By that time the problems had ended. Then in 1968, the Scrabble School was permanently closed because the other Rappahannock schools could accommodate all the county children. She completed all her schooling in the county public system. (Years later, on May 1, 2010, the Scrabble School had its grand opening as the African-American Heritage Center and the Rappahannock Senior Citizen Site.)

My younger daughter Kim started first grade in 1970 in the newly integrated Rappahannock County Elementary School in Little Washington. After the third grade she entered the Wakefield Country Day School, a private school in Huntly, and graduated from there. Some of her father's (Moody Aylor's) horse-riding clients persuaded him to send her to this private school and helped her get a scholarship. When Kim first entered Wakefield, some of the white boys would call her the N-word. But it soon became better, and she became the only girl in the boys' soccer team.

But unfortunately, some echoes of school segregation still reverberate in my family. In 1990, Janice's son Christopher Turner was enrolled in the gifted and talented program at Rappahannock High School, but he suffered in that environment. He developed anxiety when the teacher made him cry in class so often that a fellow girl student felt compelled to report the situation to his parents so, the family moved to Warrenton so he could transfer to Fauquier High School, where he did very well. He went on to Shenandoah University, then to EPCI Technical School to learn medical coding on computer. He's currently JV Coach at Wakefield Country Day in Marshall, VA.

He's also a counselor at Timber Ridge School for Boys.

These days I think schools are too lenient with students. I know, when I was in school, if we did something bad that we would get in trouble. One time, when I was in the first grade, my first cousin and I were talking, and the teacher told us to stop. We didn't stop talking, she got the ruler and slapped our hand. That was it. I didn't talk when I wasn't supposed to anymore. Or we were punished by having to stay in during recess, or write 100 times on the blackboard, "I will not talk in class or chew gum." Or we used to have to sit in the corner of the classroom. These punishments taught us right from wrong. You would be embarrassed, and you wouldn't do it again. You shame a child, and they are not going to do it again. Sometimes the teacher would send a note home and our parents would punish us too. If I talked back, I would have been smacked across the mouth. Believe me, it worked!

Our black community is just one big family. We look after each other. If one had and the other didn't, they would share. It was the same if there was a death in the family. Everybody came together and brought food and would do other things to help them out. Everyone took care of each other. And today, that just doesn't happen. I worry that if things keep going the way they have been recently, and black people keep leaving the county, the churches in Rappahannock are going to have to close their doors if we can't get new people in.

We've made real progress, but there's still work to be done. We've had a black President in the White House; we have Congressman John Lewis inspiring us from Georgia. I hope I've made my contribution to society by earning the respect of all people, white and black.

COLLEGE?

My Dad wanted me to come and stay in Plainfield, New Jersey, and go to college. There were great schools near his home.

I graduated from George Washington Carver High School 4th in my class of seventy-something and received a scholarship in the amount of $100.00. I wanted to go to Virginia Union in Richmond, VA. But I was convinced that I could not afford to go. The $100 scholarship wouldn't do me any good because it would cost a lot more than that to go to Richmond. So, I did not accept the scholarship because I decided I was not going to college.

Another reason I didn't go is that my grandmother Rosie — and I really loved her, she was the sweetest person — said, "I'm not going to tell you what to do, but I don't think you should."

She then brought up the point that my father "hasn't paid any attention to you all this time, so why does he want you to come up there and put you through school?" I listened to her, and instead of going up there to school I got married!

Many a day, I wish I would have taken a different path and gone on to college. I think about the choice I made a lot. I probably should have gone on. But my path would take me in another direction.

ME AND MOODY in his baseball uniform at Carver High School in 1956.

GETTING MARRIED

I first met Moody Aylor at a May Day at the Washington Graded School. He was probably in the 7th grade, and I was in 3rd grade. On May Days, all the students from all the schools came together and you got to meet kids from all over the county. He and I would keep meeting at various school activities over the years, and in church at the Hopewell Baptist Church in Sperryville. We were in Sunday school together too.

One May Day in 1956 at the Carver School, Moody was wearing his baseball uniform and I was in the court of the May Day Queen. I watched him play. He was a good player. He had been driving our school bus from Rappahannock to George Washington Carver High School, and even went to class there for a couple of years. He finished 9th grade when I graduated from high school.

It was probably in my junior year in high school that we started dating. We'd go down on Fletcher's Farm to go fishing and horseback riding down on the river. That's the only time I ever did any riding! He was a good teacher. His life has always been horses. In those days he didn't have horses of his own, so he had plenty of time to go to church with me.

In 1957 I got married two weeks out of school! Now that I think about it, it wasn't even two weeks. I graduated on June 11th and

MOODY AND RUSSELL AYLOR. 1957.

married on the 23rd. We just decided at the last minute that Sunday. We went to the preacher's house and got married by Elder Smith Timbers. My mom and my grandmom, his mom and some cousins were there. We had called earlier in the day and Elder Timbers wasn't home. Then we called again later, and he was home. So, we got married just before midnight!

Our honeymoon was spending the weekend at a military base near Laurel MD. Moody had enlisted in the Army for two years, from 1957 to 1959, and was going to be stationed in Germany as a private. He had gone through his basic training in North Carolina. His mother was with us too. (She had her own room!)

When we first got married, we lived in a house on Jim Bill Fletcher's farm with a cousin of my husband, and his wife Mary, right around the road from his parents. We stayed with them for about a month and then he went into the service. After Moody went into the Army, I moved back home. My mother didn't say much about it at all. Neither she or my grandmother said anything, now that I think about it.

It was pretty rough during my teenage years, and the same in my twenties. My family helped me to take care of my kids. But at that stage they weren't taking care of me, since I was married. They expected me to take care of myself and the new baby, Pete. I did a little bit of work, but mainly it was my husband's military pay that supported us. It came directly to me. I was the only person in Sperryville and Gid Brown Hollow not working, and had access to a car. So I began to be called on to take elder family members to the doctor's office and the hospital. I occasionally did housework for people.

My family liked Moody. Then, he was nice. He changed when he came back from Germany. I think he found a friend there. He kept receiving letters when he returned from Germany.

MOODY AYLOR GRADUATED from 9th grade at Carver High School. He took classes while waiting to drive the school bus back to Rappahannock. Although I was younger than him, he was my student once when I was a substitute and taught his science class.

PETE AYLOR, 1978.

*PETE AYLOR. Graduation from
Rappahannock High School .
June 9, 1978.*

*WILLIAM L. AYLOR, JR (PETE).
Marine Corp photo.*

STARTING A FAMILY

PETE

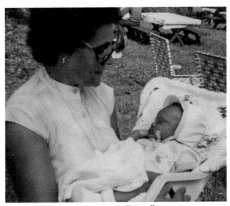

Our son William Lewis "Pete" Aylor, Jr., was born on May 25, 1958 while my husband was in Germany. He was born at the Front Royal Hospital. James "Soup" Johnson drove us to the hospital, he was one of the few people with a car who lived near us.

LILLIAN AND HER SON "Pete".

Pete was almost a year old when Moody returned from Germany. We moved in with his parents for a very short time. It was even shorter than we had expected because there was a fire. That was an amazing event. The fire started in the attic right over my baby's crib. I was at work. My sister-in-law, Rachel Aylor, was there and had her little girl there too. Pete woke up, and Rachel heard him crying and went to get him. When she got to the baby's room, she saw the fire. She got the two kids out of the room and sat them outside on the bank. She went right back in the house and the fire had broken through and fallen on the crib. It's a good thing Pete cried!

He was a good baby, very energetic. He got his name this way: Mrs. Havanna Jeffries, who owned the Pine Knot Inn, held an Easter egg roll every Easter. The winner of the roll would win a prize rabbit. When Pete was about seven years old, he won the rabbit. People started calling him "Peter Rabbit." Then they dropped the rabbit and kept the Pete.

He was a good athlete and played basketball in high school but, from childhood he was focused on the horses. He was riding horses at 3 years old. At age 6, he scared me to death when he fell off a horse on the driveway at Thornton Hill. On the drive down to the hospital in Charlottesville he didn't make a sound, until I pointed out an Army convoy. He came out of that fine! Mrs. Mary Jamison once wrote in the *Rappahannock News* that "Pete stuck to a horse saddle like a stamp."

Pete graduated from high school and joined the Marines for a couple of years. Then he came back to Virginia, and it's been racehorse training ever since, first working for his father at the races in Charles Town, WVA. He moved to a big farm in Warrenton after he

PETE AYLOR, Mr. Clifford Miller, Jr. and Cliff Yonce, 1978.

got married to his first wife, Tracy Veney from Luray. They had a daughter, Natasha, in 1986.

Tracy died in the early 1990's, and Pete remarried to Priscilla Vigay; they had a son, Joseph. After they divorced, Pete married Donna, with a daughter, Victoria Brooks. Victoria was one of my mentees when I was a mentor in the Headwaters program at Rappahannock High School.

Since that Warrenton job, Pete has worked as a jockey, but mostly he's been a horse trainer at the Charles Town Racetrack. He's had a few big successes. His daughter Tasha works with him training horses—the third generation of horse-training Aylors! Natasha was also a National Honors Student in high school.

MY GRANDSON JOSEPH AYLOR, age 12, receiving his black belt in martial arts.

MY GRANDDAUGHTER, NATASHA AYLOR, a prize winning jockey.

JANICE

JANICE AYLOR. GRADUATION 1979.

After Moody's return from Germany we had two girls. Janice was born on January 3rd, 1961. We were living on the Fletcher farm in what used to be Mr. Jim Bill Fletcher's old office building in the yard. Moody was working for Mr. Fletcher taking care of the racecourses, and training horses for the racetrack. It was a large farm with orchards. So Moody was there when Janice was about to be born and he took me to the hospital while his mother and sister looked after Pete. They lived on the Fletcher's farm too.

In those days, Pete was out with Moody all the time and I was on my own with the girls. Then Janice became crazy about horses too and started riding really young.

I worked on the farm too, looking after Mrs. Mattie Ball Fletcher who had broken her hip. She liked to do a lot of cooking and had a little oven up in her room. She was always doing things with it, so I was the one bringing her what she needed.

PETE AYLOR and sister Janice

Janice was kind of a tomboy. People started calling her Smokey Bear because she liked to climb trees. One day when she was around 8 or 9, she fell out of a tree and broke her arm, and we had to rush off to Charlottesville. From then on everyone said she was a baby bear.

Janice was in the first grade when the schools became integrated in Rappahannock. She went down to the Scrabble School. Being part of the move toward integration at school was not hard for her, or for Pete either, because they were working with horses. She already had all kinds of white friends at the barn, from New York and all over. Horse work exposed her to lots of different kinds of people.

JANICE PAGE, HER SON,
Christopher Turner & wife Keosha.

JANICE AYLOR Turner
and Haywood Turner

JANICE AYLOR PAGE
and second husband,
Calvin Lee Page.

Janice graduated from Rappahannock High School. She was good at sports— basketball, and especially field and track. She was on a good team and we went down around Richmond to compete.

Instead of going to college, she worked at Mrs. Mary Jamison's for a

JANICE'S GRANDCHILDREN:
Cecilia, Trey & Chloe Turner

while before she got married. She married Haywood Turner from Little Washington, who was a manager at the Giant supermarket in Warrenton.

Janice became a minister at Faith Christian Outreach Center in Warrenton. She also trained racehorses, like her father and brother. After Haywood passed, she lived in Warrenton where she met her second husband, Calvin Page. They bought a house in Winchester, where they moved, and then moved to a big farm near Charles Town where she could keep her five horses. She had a horse training and breeding business. Her son Christopher now lives in Cross Junction near Winchester with his wife Keosha and three children, Cecilia, Tremain, and Chloe.

Clockwise: Lillian (me), Bertha Freeman, Rosie Freeman, Janice Turner and baby Christopher Tremaine. 1984.

In 2010 Janice was diagnosed with colon cancer, which had spread. She fought it for five years, but because she'd had breast cancer before, she couldn't get any health insurance. She came to my 75th birthday party feeling pretty bad, but she put up a good front. She wouldn't let it get her down.

The week before she passed on August 29, 2015, I spent three days with her, and she said, "Mama, I'm ready to go home now."

Moody and I came to see her at the hospital on her last day. She had the biggest smile on her face, seeing us. That night Calvin called me and told me she was gone. I'm close to Christopher and my great-granddaughters and great-grandson, and it keeps me close to Janice.

In Loving Memory
A Beautiful Woman of God!

Janice Lee Page

January 3, 1961 - August 27, 2015

Service
September 2, 2015 at 11 A.M.
Enders and Shirley Funeral Home
1050 West Main Street
Berryville, VA 22611

REMEMBRANCE *of Janice Page*

My faith is the only thing that helped me get through it. Janice had a lot of faith too. She had been going to a Methodist Church when she got sick, and it was a Methodist minister who did her service. Over 300 people came to the funeral home in Berryville—luckily it was big enough that everyone could be seated. Many of the ministers from Rappahannock came. That made me feel good, to have the support of our community.

Kim Aylor

KIM

Kim was born on August 9, 1964. We were still at Fletcher's, but we moved about a month after she was born to an old log cabin on Keyser Run that Moody and his brother bought. Years earlier, when I used to walk with my grandmother to the Sneads, we would always stop there at the spring to get water to take home. It was the best cold water! We fixed up the old house and his brother built a new one. Until his death in March 2019, Moody lived at 217 Keyser Run Rd, Washington VA. And he still used that spring to get water to the house.

It was a pretty big house. When we first moved there, we didn't have running water! But I was used to that. The house I grew up in didn't have running water or indoor plumbing. And the Fletcher house also didn't have indoor plumbing. So it was nothing new.

The two older kids were big enough to be with their dad all the time. Once Kim got big enough, she was with her dad too. He had them all. She can ride, but she's an even better riding teacher. Kim was so sweet. Everybody took a liking to her. She did a lot of babysitting in high school, and when she'd leave, the kids would cry.

After the children were older, a Mr. Wells from Minnesota bought a house in Sperryville, and traveled back and forth, and hunted with the Rappahannock Hunt. Moody traveled quite a bit transporting the horse between Sperryville and Minnesota. While he was on the road, I took the children back and forth from home to the stables to take care of the horses.

Since having to spend so much time waiting for the kids, I decided to go to work for Mr. and Mrs. Fletcher until the kids were finished with their work to go home. Sometimes I would help them. I did everything but ride.

The kids were working for Moody in the barn, but I wanted them with me too. They sang in the young people's chorus at Hopewell Baptist Church, and went to perform at Wolf Trap. Moody needed them for his work, and he didn't want them to go to church because it cut down on their time to work.

Kim went to Rappahannock Elementary School till third grade. She was a little worried about leaving all her friends behind to go to the Wakefield School, but to her surprise when she got there, she soon didn't feel so all-alone.

For Kim, school was a little different experience. Janice and Pete were in the 4H club and the Scouts. But Wakefield took students on trips to travel abroad, to Germany, France and other parts of Europe. So she got to see the world.

I took Kim to piano lessons once in a while. She didn't finish but she is one of the greatest players and she did it on her own.

After Wakefield, she went to James Madison University for a couple of years, studying communications. She didn't finish because every weekend she had to come home to work for Moody. I had to go pick her up—the only weekend she didn't come home was because it snowed. Instead of finishing at James Madison, in 1990 when she was 20 years old, she went to Tulsa, OK, to the Rhema Bible Training College to prepare to become a preacher. She and Janice were singing at Bob Dumphy's church in Little Washington, and she decided to learn more about the Bible.

Soon after she got out there, she started working in the shoe

KIM WITH FAMILY. Left to right: Rev. Jeff Beard, Taylor Beard, Landrum Beard, Kim Beard (co-pastor).

department at Dillard's. She was pretty good. Then she worked at a juvenile detention center.

After two years, she came home and got a job at the Boxwood House, a substance abuse program in Culpeper. There she met her husband, Landrum Jeffrey Beard, a counselor there. Both are ordained ministers and have a non-denominational church, The Living Faith Church in Winchester. Kim worked at another youth residential treatment center in Winchester. Kim drives a school bus for the city of Winchester.

They have a son, Landrum, who is an ultimate Frisbee athlete at Mary Washington University. Their daughter Taylor Yvonne, who is now a freshman at the University of Cincinnati, OH, was a state and national high jumper in high school. They're both excellent students and athletes.

I'm proud of all of my children and grandchildren.

LANDRUM BEARD competing in Ultimate Frisbee.

TAYLOR BEARD, State and National Champion High Jumper and runner.

MOODY AND I PART WAYS

Moody and I divorced in July 1978. He and I had become different people after 20 years of marriage. He'd get mad because I went to church so much, and said I wasn't spending enough time at home. One night we had a singing group coming from Maryland to the Hopewell Church. They were late getting there because of the traffic. Moody didn't believe that I could have been in church all that time, and he got really mad and a little rough. Another time was Easter. I had gone to Charlottesville shopping and gotten a turkey for Easter dinner. I thought I'd do the cooking the night before so I could go to sunrise service the next morning. He threw a fit, and I left the house to stay with my sister-in-law Rachel. She understood what was going on.

His father was the same way. He had quite a temper.

Eventually the kids understood too. When I left, the kids went with me. But Moody had them with him during the day, working.

It was hard. He kept telling me he wanted a divorce, but he'd never do anything about it.

He was partying a lot and staying out at night, and the kids would be with him. I would have to go get them, though they didn't complain. He had several relationships with some of those people at the barn, white women. I knew about that for a while.

Back then, though, I was 40 years old at the time I had become divorced. I had been married 20 years. Financially it was a real struggle. I had to buy a car. I got all kinds of jobs in the 1970s, doing work three and four days a week, one of those days in Fairfax, Virginia. I did bookkeeping for a couple of businesses. I was a cook at a girls' camp for four summers, at Camp Roundabout on Route 231. I was assistant Girl Scout leader while Janice was in the Scouts and Kim was a Brownie. I worked for the Fletchers, babysitting at night and cooking.

My mother-in-law Lottie Aylor always considered me as her daughter. She was very supportive. When Moody and I broke up, she told me, "I know it wasn't your fault."

My two oldest children had finished high school and my son had gone in the Marines. My youngest daughter Kim had graduated from Wakefield Country Day School and gone on to James Madison University during this time. She came home every weekend to help her father with the horses, but I would be the one picking her up after class on Friday down in Harrisonburg and taking her back Sunday evening.

I needed to find a better way to support myself.

COMPUTER EDUCATION

Rappahannock News, Washington, Va.
Thursday, August 14, 1980

—Rappahannock News Photo/Daphne Hutchinson

NEW GRADUATE—Lillian Aylor of Washington received her diploma Monday night in ceremonies at the Computer Learning Center in Springfield. Currently employed as a proof operator for the Bank of Virginia, Mrs. Aylor completed a one year course in computer operations.

When my daughter Janice graduated from Rappahannock High School, Pam Williams, a friend who graduated with her, moved with her family to Alexandria. Pam's mother and father had gone to school with me and were old friends. They had built a house near us in Sperryville when they were married. One day Janice said to me, "Let's go visit Pam."

When I got down there, Pam had just come from a Computer Learning Center. She had gone over there to take a test. Unfortunately, she didn't pass the test.

She said to me, "I bet you could pass that test." That was something to think about. I immediately got on the phone and made an appointment. I went again to Alexandria and took the test, and I passed it. The counselor said my score was excellent, such as I could be a programmer or operator. But because of my age, I had to settle on being an operator.

So, in August 1978, I decided to go to the Computer Learning Center in Springfield three nights a week for one year. At that time, I was staying with my cousins, Charles and Ora Roy in Springfield — the same couple who owned their home in Gid Brown Hollow that I moved into with my children when I went through my divorce. They had two houses in Alexandria. One was rented, and I stayed in the other one, which was a new townhouse.

After a while I moved to Washington, DC, and stayed with another cousin, William Porter, Sr., and helped him, as he was having some health issues. I still went to school to learn computer operations. I graduated with honors and made appointments for a few job interviews in Washington, DC.

Well, I got over there and could not find a parking space anywhere. I looked and drove around, but still couldn't find a place to park. So, I finally went back and called them to say I wouldn't be at the interview because I couldn't find a parking space. I think it was a blessing because I didn't want to work in DC anyways. I waived my rights to a placement.

Instead, I ended up working at the Bank of Virginia in Springfield, not far from the school. While attending class I had been working at Morrow's Nut House at the Springfield Mall. I was training to be assistant manager when I heard about an opening at Bank of Virginia for a proof operator. The proof was a machine that processed the checks taken by the tellers that day. The proof caught the mistakes on the checks before they went to settlement and were cleared for payment.

I worked in the computer room starting at 8:00 p.m. with the main computer operator, after proof had finished its work and had closed. We would go in and use the computer to sort the checks and transmit them to Richmond. There was a great big machine that scanned them, and I was learning all those numbers.

One night the main operator didn't come in, and the two supervisors were all frantic and didn't know exactly what to do. They pulled me from the proof department and put me in the computer room and started asking questions about how to make the transfers to Richmond. I was just in training and thought, "Oh my Lord, what have I gotten myself into?" But we got through it and they told everyone what I had done. It went into my personnel file. I felt so good about that evening.

THE BEAUTIFUL Blue Ridge I call home.

COMING HOME TO RAPPAHANNOCK
AND MT. VERNON FARM

I was on my way to the bank one Monday morning and I went down to the stables to see my ex-husband Moody who was taking care of Mr. Miller's horses. Mr. J. Clifford Miller Jr. was owner of the Mount Vernon Stock Farm in Sperryville. He had just finished riding.

He asked what I was doing. I told him I was working at the Bank of Virginia as a proof operator, but I would love to get back home. "Oh, you would? Why don't you come over and talk to Mrs. Miller and me this weekend." I sat down with them on Sunday evening and they gave me a job.

I went to the bank on Monday and turned in my resignation, and then started working Mt. Vernon Farm on the 5th of January 1981, and I am still here 38 years later.

In those days, the Miller family lived in Richmond and came up to Rappahannock on weekends. At first, I became the bookkeeper and did the payroll for the farm, and I did the housekeeping. I also cooked for them when they were at the farm. When they needed parts for the tractor, I'd go down to Orange to pick them up. I did so much running around, they even paid for my gas.

I was still living in Gid Brown Hollow. Kim was going to James

Madison University, and Janice was getting ready to get married and she wasn't spending much time at home. The Millers were calling me at home so often they paid my phone bill. Mrs. Lizora Miller was especially generous, and always had a little something extra for me in the middle of the year. We were very close. When she was sick and resting in the living room, she took my hand and said she hoped that, as long as she lived, I would always be with her. At her funeral service, I sang "Just a Closer Walk with Thee" for her; at Mr. Miller's, I sang "Precious Lord, Take My Hand."

In 1989, Mr. and Mrs. Miller, Jr., built me a house on the Mt. Vernon Farm on Water Street in Sperryville. My mother was getting on in age and not well, so I took her in with me.

And then in 2005, my aunt Margaret Freeman Poles was living alone, and when it snowed it was almost impossible to get to her to take her to her doctor's appointments. Some of her white neighbors, the Beahms, helped out by calling her, and one particular time, Carolyn Beahm walked in the snow to see about her—and the snow was deep!

At the end of the winter I took Margaret to come live with me until the last year of her life, when her Alzheimer's got so bad that she moved to the Jackson House Assisted Living Center in Boston, VA. She did not get enough Social Security to take care of her medical bills. When she passed in March 2012, Cliff Miller III helped me pay them off.

After her husband Uncle Haywood died in 1993, Aunt Margaret and I spent much time together and became closer, getting groceries, taking her back and forth to the doctors. We often talked about family things I had not heard before. Before that I didn't really know much about my family origins. I knew my father looked white. That's all I knew. But then my grandmother, his mother, she also looked white. I guess she really was.

In 2001 and 2002, my mother-in-law Lottie Aylor agreed to let Cliff Miller III interview her about her life. He and I would drive together to her home and spend about an hour listening and learning. In all there were four taped interviews. Early on in our first interview, Lottie told him about her understanding that her grandfather was white, and the impact that had on her life. That day, on our drive home from the interview he expressed surprise. I told him, "Yes, and I am pretty much the same as Lottie." I explained that I had heard that my grandfather was a distant cousin of his. This was another surprise to him, but we agreed it could be true. Only recently did my DNA test show that was not accurate.

Then one Thanksgiving Day around the year 2000, I was in the kitchen at Mount Vernon Farm, making the Thanksgiving dinner. Thanksgivings were a major time when all the Miller family and assorted relatives got together, and it was a big deal! I had the challenge of preparing the meals, and Lottie made sure she was invited to come help, even when she was only able to sit down and oversee. Just like every year, we started the day with a special egg and sausage casserole for breakfast. For dinner around 7 pm, we had hors d'oeuvres.

There was a huge turkey, mashed potatoes and gravy, maybe a leg of lamb, peas and carrots, a romaine lettuce salad with balsamic vinegar dressing. I would make molded cranberry sauce. We had my ham biscuit and dinner rolls. Mr. Cliff Miller, Jr., really loved applesauce and buckwheat cakes every morning; they would buy the buckwheat flour in Stratford Hall, the home of Robert E. Lee's parents in Stratford, VA.

For dessert, we always had oatmeal raisin cookies and some little teeny lemon tarts. Children loved vanilla ice cream. I always made a birthday cake for Clay Yonze, Cliff's nephew whose birthday is also on or around Thanksgiving. Everything was homemade, except the ice cream!

That afternoon I was getting things ready for dinner. All of the Miller family was in the living room awaiting Lottie and me to climb the stairs and join the blessing of the dinner, and for me to sing "Amazing Grace". As I was going up, I heard Cliff III telling the rest of the family, "It looks like Lillian could be related to us."

I was shocked at him telling them that way. It was a little embarrassing but at the time I believed it was true. I turned around and went back downstairs. The Millers and I have always been close, so that news didn't seem to change anything.

A TANGLED MYSTERY

In 2019, my family's story got a lot more complicated. Since I was writing my memoir, I thought I should just go ahead and take a DNA test. When I got the results from two tests—one from Ancestry.com and another from 23 and Me—I was shocked to discover a whole new group of relatives, the Smedleys and the Finchams, that I never knew I had. What's more, at 80 years old, I had to let go of who I thought my grandfather—my father's father—was, and with that our blood relation to the Millers. It turns out that pictures and family stories, even handwritten records in cookbooks and family bibles, don't always tell the real story. Yet in photos my father looks so much like my "grandfather" Brooke Miller. Even the ears matched!

I had been working with Jan McKinney, a local genealogist in Rappahannock, to draw up my family tree. She's the one who figured out that my link to the Miller family is not what I thought it was. She's from around here too and is a Fincham. One day she announced to me with surprise that the DNA results show that my great-grandfather was a Fincham too. That means she and I are cousins! And so is her stepfather, C.E. Dodson!

Then in July of 2019, I got an email from Craig Smedley of Springfield OH, who by coincidence had just done his DNA. Craig, who is 51 years old and white, announced to me that we were related through my grandfather Arthur Freeman. He's my 4th to 6th cousin! He said his great-grandfather was mulatto and married a white woman. He gave me more information than I even knew.

Here's what he wrote:

> "Crazy coincidence, I guess. Yes they are my relatives. There are many Smedleys that you and I share as relatives. Even some without the Smedley name are Smedleys. For example, Rexette Warner, Gerald Herrmann, Tammy Coor, Anthony Milano and others. All of these people are descended from my 2X great-grandfather and probably most of them show up as matches with you. So we likely shared a grandparent from around 1800. Or my 2X great-grandfather, born in 1828, is a sibling of one of your grandparents. It is a tangled mystery. I believe that my 2X great-grandfather went by the name William King when he was in Rappahannock in 1850. I believe he was the mulatto that lived with the McFarlings (McFarland) on the 1850 census. I believe he changed his name to Smedley because his biological grandfather was William Smedley born in the 1700s, and William Smedley had a (biological) daughter named Tabitha "Smidley" (Smedley) that married a King. I believe Tabitha was a free person of color as she appears living alone on a couple of census records. Of course it will take a miracle to prove this. ☺"

Now that I think of it, I remember Jimbo Smedley, a character who lived nearby when I was a girl. He had cows that were always out on our road. He also made moonshine at this house and got caught. They made him tear the still down, so he went higher up the mountain and built another. I think my great–grandfather Fincham might have called him a cousin. Years later, Roger Flinchum, who was a teacher at the Rappahannock High School, bought Jimbo's place and found his old still. Roger was my son Pete's teacher.

My family sure is a tangled mystery. It shows how slavery created mixed bloodlines between African-Americans and whites, whether people admitted it or not, and how complicated and sometimes tragic it could be for families. Using DNA to trace these lines has broadened my sense of family and community here in Rappahannock, reaching as far away as Ohio, and maybe even further. We're all related! Jan is still trying to find out all the connections, especially the identity of my father's father. You can read her report on my family tree at the back of this book in Appendix IV.

By another coincidence, my granddaughter Taylor Beard will be starting as a freshman at the University of Cincinnati in the fall of 2019. Now she'll have her cousin Craig Smedley nearby to visit!

Singing at the John Jackson Blues Festival at Eldon Farm, Woodville, 2019

CHURCH LIFE AND THE
SCRABBLE SCHOOL

Promised Land Baptist Church in Washington Va. was my church growing up, and central to our community. It made me a faithful churchgoer all my life. But we also visited each other's churches all through the year, especially at Homecomings, which were held on different Sundays so we could get to them all. That included First Baptist Church in Washington, where I got my start in singing in public, doing solos and recitations. I've been the pianist there since 2003.

Just before I got married, Moody and I used to go to Sunday School at Hopewell. After we were married, I sang in the choir and worked with the missionary society. Hopewell and Promised Land were members of the Baptist General Convention in Richmond, which organizes missionary work in jails, helping foster children, and other important community work all over Virginia.

My brother Forrest was a pastor for a while at the Bethel Baptist Church in Amissville, and we used to attend their revivals and homecomings every year. For a number of years I went to their Watch Night Services to watch the old year go out and the New Year come in. We'd have dinner there at 9 p.m. in their basement dining room. At 10:30 we'd go up to have a service until midnight. There would be singing and preaching and testimonies. I really liked those services; they were inspirational. You're thankful that you'd made it through another year!

My mother and grandmother Rosie used to attend Mount Moriah Baptist in Amissville for their homecomings, way back. And now I'm going there for ushers' meetings. They have guest singers sometimes.

I go to Shiloh Baptist in Woodville, near where I live, to their homecomings and revivals to sing. I was pianist at Shiloh for a time. We loved the pastor, Reverend Tinsley, who died recently. He was jovial and you could talk to him. At times I felt more comfortable talking to him than my own pastor!

Macedonia Baptist in Flint Hill is like the others. Their Homecoming is in July, and their revivals take place the week leading up to the third Sunday in July. It's a big church, with members coming from as far as Strasburg.

Revivals used to last five days when I was a girl, sometimes with different preachers on different days. Here in Rappahannock, we've cut it down to three nights. The point is to revive our spirit and our faith, with a meeting, preaching and singing. Then they open the doors of the church for those who don't belong, or who want to revive their fellowship. For newcomers, there were baptisms, with full immersion in water. Sometimes these happen in a river. Macedonia has its own pool inside the church.

There were two "old-school" Baptist churches. One was in Huntly, where my mother and grandmother went. The other was in Harris Hollow, which was destroyed in a flood. Our homecoming at Promised Land used to be on the fourth Sunday in August. The old-school people started coming to Promised Land, so Promised

Land changed its homecoming to September to accommodate them. Both old-school churches have died down since then. They were strict and didn't use instrumental music. Instead they sang metered hymns—a kind of call and response in which a member would say the words, and then the congregation would sing them.

***

LOTTIE AYLOR and Rev. Charles Sims at Wayland Blue Ridge Baptists Association Center, 2003.

Church life has always been important to me, and is probably more important to me now that I am in my senior years and living alone. I know it is only through the grace of God that I am still as healthy and active as I am. When my daughter Janice was 53 and diagnosed with stage 4 colon cancer that spread to her liver, the tumors were growing so fast on her intestines that there was a blockage where food and drink would not stay down. She was denied any type of treatments because she had no health insurance. All medications she got had to be paid for up front. I know the Lord gave me my job and the strength to provide for her as much as I could. And some really good friends through the church made it possible to get her medications.

In October 2013, my daughter Kim and niece Cristol Porter gave a 75th birthday party for me at the Sperryville Fire hall. I had asked that all gifts that were going to be given to me go to my daughter Janice. You would not believe the outpouring of gifts given to Janice and me, over $3000 to help with her medical bills. Faith has a lot to do with it, but also the caring community too. I really felt loved and

My 75th Birthday Celebration at the Sperryville Firehouse, 2013. Top *photo:*
Me and my nieces, nephews, and in-laws. bottom photo: *Me and my extended family of*
children, grandchildren, brothers and sisters.

supported. The church and my faith also give me the chance to help people when I can. That is a real gift.

Today I'm in four or five choirs. At my church now, the Promised Land Baptist Church, believe it or not, we used to have a full choir. Now I am the only member. Back in 2000 when we celebrated Promised Land's 100th anniversary, the choir box was full. Now it is totally different. We have a declining population as people die, and no African-Americans are moving in. We are down to sometimes 20 people, most times it's even less. And in Little Washington, where we used to have a big choir, now we only have three people. Down at Woodville they have a big choir but low attendance.

If it weren't for the Unity Choir, which I pretty much organized and has seven or eight churches involved, we wouldn't have any choirs. The Unity Choir fills in, going on engagements with my Pastor, Reverend Herbert Johnson of Promised Land Baptist, and with his nephew Reverend Ronald Johnson of Hopewell Baptist,

THE UNITY CHOIR performs at the John Jackson Blues Festival at Eldon Farms, Woodville, 2019.

and with Reverend Kilby of First Baptist Washington. We have even gone with my brother, Rev. Forrest Freeman, when he didn't have a choir to go with him.

I've also been a member of the Wayland Blue Ridge Baptist Association Choir in Rixeyville since 1972. I am a member of the Ministers and Deacons Union Choir, also the Women's Auxiliary Choir. We used to have 52 churches, but now we're down to 30 or so. I've served as our Financial Secretary from 1997 to 2003. And then 2003-2004 I served as Treasurer. Now I'm done with that part, but I'm still in the choirs.

I think churches need to come together. That is one of my concerns. We have four black Baptist churches right here in Rappahannock. The Hopewell Baptist in Sperryville finally has a pastor. But the congregations are getting too small to support them. Young people aren't coming—when they graduate, they leave the county.

I said to them, "You all are going to end up closing the doors. You all can't support this church." The reason is they have big heating and cooling bills, along with insurance. One solution might be for the pastors and congregations to share a rotating schedule with one service at each church per month, with all parishioners attending each service.

In my own family people have left the county to look for work. In the same way, it hurts me so much to see this happening in the local black churches. When we were growing up we walked to church. We had a lot of fun at night revivals and other programs. Now revivals only last Thursdays to Friday, with Homecoming on Sunday, instead of the whole week leading to Sunday. The road would be full of young people. We had a good time. Most of those young people have died and others have moved out of the county. You know, we just don't have enough people left.

Besides my church work and my job at The Inn at Mount Vernon, I keep very busy working in community organizations to preserve our history. The Rappahannock Historical Society, located on Gay Street in Little Washington, has pretty extensive files on the development of the county, and it publishes books. At first, the Society's records seemed to exclude the black history of the county. No African-Americans had been asked to join.

Then Wayne Baldwin, who's white, was a pretty good friend and a member, asked me to join because he wanted more African-Americans involved. I originally joined around 2003 to do some research on my ancestors. I wish I had more time to spend there! Today I am on the board and serve as treasurer. Some time ago, I gave them an oral history of my community that is kept in their archives. Now I'm pleased that anyone in the future will be able to find information about my ancestors and theirs at the Society.

I am on the board of the Scrabble School African-American Preservation Foundation and have been Vice President since 2003. We started it because we felt we needed a place to keep our records. Frank Warner had gone to the Scrabble School as a child and then moved to Washington, DC. When he came back, he was shocked to see the condition the school was in, trash in the yard, all grown up, it was awful. He started a Foundation and worked to restore the building and the grounds. When he died in 2003, his wife and Bob Lander took it on.

The Scrabble School is the closest to my heart because it is keeping the heritage going and it brings back a lot of memories about the way things were. Even though the black population is dwindling, in many ways African-Americans built this community and our contribution needs to be remembered.

Over the years I've served as Vice-president and Treasurer from 2003 to 2015, and now I'm the Treasurer.

The four great African-American teachers in the Rappahannock Rosenwald School system—Miss Carol Williams and Miss BeeBee Austin, Miss Boddie and Dorothy Butler—changed many lives, including mine. Their memory needs to be honored and records kept.

Our goal at the Scrabble School Foundation is to preserve historical artifacts. We have put documents on microfilm and a person can look up the information. We are currently raising money for a new monitor to make it easier to read. It would be great to be able to go there and press a button and see all the history.

Even though you can't stop change and nothing stays the same, it's important to remember what used to be.

***

There *are* important social service organizations in the county that I contribute to. I've been secretary of the Rappahannock Convalescent Loan Closet, which collects medical equipment to lend out to people in need—wheelchairs, walkers, canes, crutches, toilet seats, shower benches. Just call me and I'll get something for you!

***

I'm *not* usually much into political stuff, but I knew that blacks were being kept away from the polls. So I was an election official for over 35 years. Around 1975 when Jimmy Carter was President, Mrs. Mildred Fletcher suggested I should start doing it. I've been doing it ever since. Once I had to work the Republican primary, and Mr. Lester Deal had something to say about that, with me not being a Republican. Mr. Tom Junk, a local antique dealer who was also Republican, came to my rescue. I resigned a few years ago.

***

I've been awarded various honors and recognition for my work in the community. In 2007, I was designated a Black Pearl in recognition for community service by the Wayland Blue Ridge Baptist Women's Auxiliary.

Then in November 28, 2013, I was a Citizen of the Year in the *Rappahannock News*! I was shocked when I found out. I couldn't believe it. But yet somehow, I had a feeling. I don't know how to explain it. Seems as if I have intuitions. The Lord is going to shows me something that is going to happen. The older I get the more I seem to know things before they actually happen.

But as I said, I was shocked. When my daughter read off all the things I have done and the organizations I have been in, everyone started saying it made them tired just hearing all the things. Cliff Miller said, "I thought you worked for me full time. When did you have time for all of these things?"

I told him, "Cliff, remember, this is over 75 years!" (You can read the article in Appendix III.)

Then in 2016, "Aging Together, Five over Fifty" gave me a service award. Aging Together is a grant program to develop services for seniors in need in five counties. Each year, they select someone from each of those five counties for their contribution to all aspects of the community. I am grateful for the award.

I have spent my life getting things done, but I have slowed down a little now. I don't do it for the notoriety, but I do hope that after I have "gone home" I will be remembered as having done something and helped many as I travel through this land of sorrow. I often don't feel deserving of all the things they are saying now.

A14 April 14, 2016   HOWDY, NEIGHBOR • FROM PAGE ONE

Lillian Aylor:
One of Aging Together's Five Over Fifty

By Staff/contributed reports

Don't let Lillian Aylor's small stature and quiet voice fool you. When she sees a need she starts working on it until something has been accomplished. In 2013 Aylor was recognized as Rappahannock Citizen of the year for the many and varied ways in which she has contributed to the community. The headline in the Rappahannock News announcing her award summed it up: "Lillian Aylor: I'll do it."

Now she's been nominated for Aging Together's Five Over Fifty Award, which recognizes the work and community impact of five individuals, one from each of the five counties served by Aging Together—Rappahannock, Fauquier, Culpeper, Orange, and Madison. Aylor and the other awardees will be honored on Saturday, April 16 at the State Theatre in Culpeper.

See AYLOR, Page A14

AYLOR
From Page A1

A caretaker to many, even when she was in need herself, a doer, someone concerned about bridging the past and the future are all reasons Lillian Aylor was nominated for the award.

Aylor's contributions to the community include serving as secretary of the Rappahannock Convalescent Loan Closet, Sperryville-Piedmont electoral official, captain of the "Spiritual Walkers" Relay for Life team, treasurer of the Rappahannock Historical Society and vice president of the Scrabble School Preservation Foundation.

She also has served on fundraising and steering committees and as a mentor for the Headwaters Foundation; raised money door-to-door for the American Red Cross and volunteered with the Rappahannock unit of the American Heart Association.

When told that she would be given one of Aging Together's Five Over Fifty awards this year Aylor asked an unsurprising question: "What about the other people who do so much?"

serving as its president and vice president. She also has been a vice chair of the Rappahannock Democratic Committee. If that wasn't enough she created and continues to support the Boddie scholarship program.

But if you ask Aylor about being a leader in the county, she instantly begins to shake her head no. She sees herself as just one of many who work together to make things happen. When told that she would be given one of Aging Together's Five Over Fifty awards this year she asked

an unsurprising question: "What about the other people who do so much?"

Aylor credits her family's values, instilled in her while growing up, for what motivates her to do so much. She also loves Rappahannock County. When work has taken her away to places like Washington, D.C., she's always been happy to return to this area. She would like to see Rappahannock as a place where children can and want to stay as they grow up. And she remembers the time when more people of color lived in the county and owned homes and farms.

"No matter what she is talking about, Aylor always finds a way back to her own children and her grandchildren, sharing their successes, their individual interests and gifts. She has been documenting her family's history with several collaborators and hopes to have it published in the near future. Her story is a picture of a life lived through

much change, some loss, and hard work. But she remains optimistic and says she's slowed down a little, although it's clear that she's still giving back a lot.

She doesn't do all the work she does for recognition. She does it because she loves it here and wants to make this a better place for people now and in the future. And that's what's at heart of the Five Over Fifty recognition.

Honorees from the other counties include Joan Proctor from Culpeper, Karen Hughes White from Fauquier, Jack and John Fray from Madison, and Robert Hall from Orange.

The award ceremony is Saturday, April 16 at the State Theatre in Culpeper. The reception begins at 5:30 p.m., and awards will be presented at 6 p.m. Tickets can be purchased at www.agingtogether.org and include a ticket to the State Theatre's concert which is an evening of music by Johnny and June Carter Cash.

RAPPAHANNOCK NEWS ARTICLE *about me getting the Aging Together Service Award.*

MY RAPPAHANNOCK JOURNEY

In the eight decades that I've lived in Rappahannock County, it's become a very different place.

As I've said earlier, my black community in the county has dwindled. Before the Civil War, about half the population of Rappahannock was slaves, with 300 to 400 freed blacks. It was still about half African-American when I was a girl. That was not so long ago.

Of the 7,400 people living in the county in 2017, 92% are white. Only 4% are black. There are few jobs. Many African-Americans can't afford the taxes and have had to let their houses go. When my aunt and uncle's house went up for sale, I was thinking of buying out the other heirs and purchasing the house myself. I decided I couldn't afford it because the taxes are around $4,000 for the year. Many can't afford a house in Rappahannock. There are a lot of wealthy retirees moving in that make the prices go up. Half the county is over 50 years old. It is very sad.

In the past, black farmers were pushed off their land by force. For example, in 1945 the Rappahannock County School Board was looking to buy land to establish a Regional High School for the white children. This plan did not have the colored children in mind. Mr. Robert Russell was approached and requested that he sell his land for that purpose. He responded that he wanted to keep his land, as his son James would be returning home soon from serving in the war overseas. His plan was to clear it and put it under cultivation. Mr. Russell's plea was met with the threat that unless he sold the acreage to them, condemnation proceedings would be instituted against him, and he would be forced to sell at below the $50-per-acre price the board was offering. G. Tyler Miller was superintendent at the time.

Mr. Robert Russell was a teacher at the Smedley Graded School for 33 years and had been my mother's teacher. James Russell, his son, showed me the letters from his father begging them not to take his land. He spoke of the sense of betrayal his father felt from the system he had so faithfully served, working to instill the values of honesty, ethics and some feeling of human dignity in his students. That land had been part of the black community, across Lee Highway from Little Washington. Now, black students would have to pass by it to get to their school in Culpeper County.

But today some things are better. There's more closeness between people of different races. In the old days, segregation separated people. I don't feel that so much anymore. There are still African-American children growing up here. This year we gave four Boddie scholarships for college, two to African-American students. Those two were from the same family and were the only black graduates of that year. They'll go off to college. That's a huge improvement from my day.

The county is still very beautiful, with a comprehensive plan to protect our natural resources. The houses we live in are healthier and more comfortable. We have phones, plumbing, clean water, and electricity everywhere. It wasn't until the mid-1980s that Sperryville had a sewer system!

I've had a good life here in spite of having been discriminated against early on in my life. I rose above it all. I did not let discrimination define me. It's not who I am. I do think that it was unfair that when I graduated from Computer School at 40 years old, I had to be a computer operator, even though my test scores were such that I could have been a programmer. They said I did not have enough years before retirement to move up the corporate ladder. But I wanted to come back to Rappahannock. If I had become a programmer and pursued a career, there would have been no job for me here, and I wouldn't have been able to come home.

It wasn't intended for me to be there.

So, who am I? I'm part African-American and part white. My DNA test shows that I'm 49.9% sub-Saharan African and 48% European, of which about a quarter is British and Irish with a little French, German and Spanish. And 1.4% Native American, thanks to my grandma Rosie. I am called black or African-American, but personally I still prefer the term "Colored." To be called black, I think, creates more separation. I'm an American, a Virginian, and from Rappahannock County.

I think it is very important to know who you are. My nephew Nils Aylor is married to a white woman. Since there are many interracial marriages these days, it seems like young people don't want to know their history. Kids now-a-days say they have arrived. But I ask, "How did they arrive?"

You tell them things about the past, they respond with, "Oh Aunt Lillian, that was a long time ago, that's not now." When young black people don't know about their heritage, they don't know where they came from, what their ancestors had to go through to get to where they are now, they can repeat the mistakes of the past.

I tell young people now that they have the opportunity to complete high school and go to college or technical school. But you have to work and apply yourself. You have to have faith and motivation. At church at our usher's anniversary, I spoke about how my daughter Janice was diagnosed with advanced colon cancer just around the time I was diagnosed with lupus. And I said to the Lord, "I'm ready to give up. I can't take any more." And He spoke to me and said that I was in His will. That he had more for me to do, and that I wasn't going to give up because there was more to do.

And now His will is probably for me to be writing this book. I have to keep going and not give up!

When I was in high school, I wanted to be either a legal secretary or a CPA. I went to night school to be an accountant, but as it turned out, I just needed more diversity in what I did for a job. I like to do a lot of different things. At 80, I am still working. I've been on this one job for 38 years, promoted in 2011 to the Innkeeper for the Inn at Mount Vernon Farm. Now I am the cook. They tried to get me to work less hours, but I'm still going strong. I live alone with my little dog, Jasmine. My financial circumstances are much better than at any other time in my life, and I'm even able to help my daughter with her expenses.

Yet after all this work, I'm starting to have some health concerns. I have a leaky left heart valve, which causes edema in hot weather, my feet and ankles swell; osteoporosis; rheumatoid arthritis; lupus; and a disintegrating disc in the lower part of my back. But so far, I am not in too much pain with these ailments and can manage it with medication.

I love this job. Every day if I didn't wake up in the morning up knowing that I have work to do, I probably would not get out of bed. I am taking care of myself by working.

About my children, I'm happy with the way they turned out. They have the best qualities of Moody and me. They're all hard workers and their children too. They're gifted and high achieving athletes like their dad, and good teachers and trainers. They're also charming like their dad and can get along with everyone.

All of them also did really well in school, like me. And like me, my two daughters became strong voices in the church, each of them becoming ordained ministers and giving back to the community as I have done. The churches I grew up in were the foundation of our community. It's been that way since after the Civil War, when churches provided a safe haven for freed slaves. It's where we turned for support and help and companionship.

I think it's important to share with others and support those less fortunate. Even though I can't afford it, if I know someone needs money, I just give it. I don't even think about it, I just do, and do without something myself. People have helped me in my time of need, and what goes around comes around, as I've said.

***

When I started this story, I think I was a little embarrassed to talk about my life. I've thought of myself as a shy person who just wants to get along.

But now it's become a release to get all this story out in the open. It's been a relief to share the details that have been kind of secret for all these years. It turns out that most people already knew most of these things!

After all, I can see that with all I've done, I'm a stronger person than I thought. And that I'm loved. I have a birthday note from Lizora Miller in 2002:

Dearest Lillian,

> *Many happy returns of your birthday, but may you always spend it with us at Mount Vernon Farm. You are a good friend and we love you.*

> *Blessings,*

Lizora Miller.

And that's why I'm at the Inn at Mount. Vernon Farm still today. It's only a few miles away from where my journey started in Gid Brown Hollow. From the Inn on Turkey Mountain, I can see the whole valley over to the Little Jenkins Mountain in Gid Brown Hollow where I grew up. The village of Sperryville is visible through the trees—the town where my children grew up and went to school, where Moody ran his riding school and taught our kids about horses, over to the Hopewell Church where I sang in the choir, and below, to the place where my house stands today along the Thornton River not far from the old Schoolhouse.

I grew up on a hill, with farmland cleared of trees. I could see the children walking down the hill to pick up the school bus on the way to school, just like I can see them today. The mountains are all around us, changing from season to season. The fall is my favorite season. I like spring too, with all the flowers, but I just love the change in the colors of the leaves on the rolling hills in the fall. I love the smell, the cool breezes after the hot summers. Some things don't change.

I'm so happy as an innkeeper to welcome journeyers to my beautiful Rappahannock County home.

A FAMILY REUNION AT MOODY AYLOR'S FUNERAL. Reynold's Memorial Baptist Church, Sperryville, April 2019.

1ST ROW left to right- Pete Aylor, Lillian Aylor, Kimberly Beard, Naveah Blankey. 2ND ROW- Brandi Beard, Tasha Beard and Jamari Darsect, Natasha Aylor, Joseph Aylor and Quita Beard. 3RD ROW- Keosha Turner, Taylor Beard, Jeff, Beard. 4TH ROW- Christopher Turner, CalvinPage, Marquis Raines and Landrum Beard.

RECIPES

FROM THE INN AT

MOUNT VERNON

FARM

LILLIAN'S BLUEBERRY FLAPJACK PUDDING

(Perfect for leftover pancakes!)

12 blueberry pancakes, cut in half

6 eggs

¾ C heavy cream

¼ C sugar

2 tbsp melted butter

1 tsp vanilla

dash cinnamon

extra blueberries, or raisins or craisins if you like

Grease casserole dish. Layer the pancakes around dish and on top of each other, adding extra blueberries (or raisins) between layers.

Whisk eggs. Whisk in milk, sugar, butter, vanilla and cinnamon. Pour mixture over pancakes and let set an hour or two or overnight, until the pancakes have soaked up the egg mixture.

Bake at 350°F for 25-30 minutes or until slightly browned and mixture is no longer runny.

Serve with syrup or a sauce of your choice.

Serves 6-8

The Inn At Mount Vernon Farm
HOMEMADE GRANOLA

4 C rolled oats

1/3 C cashews

1/3 C sunflower seeds

1 C slivered or chopped almonds

¾ C dried apricots

1 C raisins or craisins

½ tsp cinnamon

¼ tsp nutmeg

2/3 stick unsalted butter

1/3 C agave nectar

Heat oven to 350°F.

Mix nuts, apricots, raisins, nutmeg and cinnamon together in a bowl.

Melt butter and add the agave to it and pour over the nuts and fruits in the bowl.

Line baking pan or broiling pan with parchment paper, pour the mixed nuts and fruits and bake about 25 minutes.

Let cool before packing in an airtight container.

Makes about 8 cups of granola.

AMISH CORNCAKE PANCAKES

1 1/3 C buttermilk

¾ C yellow corn meal

1 tsp. baking powder

¼ tsp. baking soda

¼ C flour

1 tsp. salt

1 tsp. sugar

1 egg

1 Tbsp. corn or olive oil

Whisk together buttermilk and baking soda and let sit for 5 minutes.

Beat egg slightly, stir in oil and add dry ingredients.

Add buttermilk mixture. The batter will be very thin.

On a hot skillet, drop heaping tablespoon of batter. Cook 1½ minute on the on the first side, and 1 minute on the bottom side.

Serve hot with maple syrup. They don't need butter!

Makes 12 pancakes

LILLIAN'S SOUTHERN BISCUITS

2 C flour

½ tsp. salt

¼ tsp. baking soda

3 tsp. baking powder

1 tsp. sugar

½ C lard

¾ C buttermilk

Heat oven to 425°F.

Sift together the flour, baking powder, soda, salt and sugar. Cut in the lard until the mixture resembles coarse crumbs.

Add buttermilk and mix quickly to bring the dough together.

Turn onto a lightly floured surface. Knead a few times to make a soft dough. Don't over-knead, or the biscuits will turn out hard and dry.

Bake at 425°F until golden brown, about 10 minutes.

Makes 6 to 24 biscuits

ITALIAN EGG & SAUSAGE CASSEROLE

(Assemble the casserole a day ahead.)

½ lb. sweet Italian sausage, lamb or pork

6 eggs, beaten

3 peppers (red, green and yellow)

4 green onions with tops, chopped

¼ zucchini, chopped (optional)

8 oz. low-fat cottage cheese

½ lb. shredded cheese
    (Monterey Jack or Mexican Four-cheese, or both)

½ tsp. baking powder

2 Tbsp. melted butter

Pull apart the sausage into small pieces and place in a skillet. Cook over medium heat until brown. Remove the sausage from the skillet and set it aside. Save the sausage fat.

Add the peppers and onions (add zucchini if using) into the skillet and sauté in the reserved fat, adding a little olive oil if needed.

In a medium bowl, add whisk the eggs.

In a small bowl, add baking powder to the melted butter and whisk into the eggs.

Add cottage cheese and shredded cheese to eggs, and mix together. Add meat and veggies and mix together.

Pour into a greased 6-by-9-inch casserole dish and refrigerate overnight.

Remove from refrigerator at least an hour before baking. Preheat the oven to 350°F.

Bake for 25 to 30 minutes.

Serves 6

DELICIOUS HUNGARIAN LAMB HASH

1 lb. cooked lamb stew meat or kabobs (grass-fed)

1 bay leaf

¾ tsp. salt

¼ tsp. black pepper

1 tsp. ground sage

1 large or 2 medium onions, sliced

4 large organic potatoes, peeled and cut into 1-inch cubes

6 slices natural uncured bacon

1 tsp. Hungarian paprika

4 eggs, preferably pastured

Place the lamb meat in a pan with just enough water to cover. Add a bay leaf, salt, pepper, sage. Cover and cook until stick-tender.

Let cool and cut into small cubes.

Place the bacon in a cold 12-inch cast-iron frying pan. On medium heat, cook the bacon, turning as necessary, until most of the fat has rendered. The bacon should be fairly crisp. Remove the bacon and safe the fat.

Add sauté onions over medium heat for 4 minutes. Stir in paprika and cook for 4 more minutes.

Add potatoes and sauté for 5 minutes. Turn heat low, cover and cook over low heat 5 minutes.

Add meat and sauté until browned, 3 to 4 minutes.

Crumble the reserved bacon and stir into the dish.

Carefully break the eggs over the hash and cook until yolks have just set. Or serve with eggs fried over easy.

Serves 10

TURKEY MOUNTAIN WILD TURKEY

I used this recipe to cook a turkey killed on Mount Vernon Farm by Cliff Miller's nephew, Clay Yonce.

One whole wild turkey, around 22 lbs., cleaned for roasting

4 apples, cored and quartered

3 carrots, halved

4 stalks celery, halved

3 onions, halved

3 9½-oz boxes of powdered milk

1½ Tbsp. baking soda

Nature's Seasons seasoning blend

In a large sink or basin, cover the turkey with water into which the powdered milk has been added. Add baking soda. Soak for 24 hours. Remove turkey and wash thoroughly with clean water.

Preheat oven to 325°F.

Rub the inside of the turkey with seasoning and black pepper. Stuff the turkey with the apples, carrots, celery and onions. Place inside a roasting pan.

Roast for 4 hours, basting every hour while cooking.

Remove from the oven when roasting thermometer reads 165°F. Cover with foil and let set for 15 minutes before carving.

LILLIAN'S SPICED NUTS

Can be stored in an airtight container for two weeks.

1 lb. (4 C) mixed unsalted nuts (cashews, almonds, walnuts, pecans)

½ tsp. ground coriander

½ tsp. ground cumin

2 Tbsp. unsalted butter

2 Tbsp. dark brown sugar

2 Tbsp. fresh rosemary, chopped

¼ tsp. cayenne pepper

1½ tsp. kosher salt

Position the rack in the center of the oven and heat to 350°F.

Scatter the nuts on a rimmed baking sheet and bake, shaking the sheets a couple of times during baking, until the nuts are nicely browned, 10 to 15 minutes.

Meanwhile in a small cast-iron skillet over medium heat, sprinkle coriander and cumin and toast until aromatic, about 30 seconds.

Take skillet off the heat and add butter, brown sugar, rosemary and cayenne. Return skillet to low heat and stir until the sugar dissolves, 2 to 2½ minutes. Keep warm.

Place the nuts in a large warmed bowl, pour in the spiced melted butter and sugar, and stir, adding the salt, until thoroughly coated.

BLACKBERRY BROWNIES

2 squared unsweetened chocolate, melted and cooled

½ C unsalted butter, softened

1 C granulated sugar

2 eggs, lightly beaten

½ C white flour

1 C walnuts, chopped

½ C blackberry jam

Heat oven to 350°F. Butter a 9-inch square baking pan.

In separate bowls, mix the wet and dry ingredients, except for the jam. Mix the batter together and pour into the baking pan. Use a spatula to smooth the batter.

Drop the jam by teaspoons into the batter. Swirl the jam with a fork to incorporate it into the batter.

Bake for 25 minutes. Then cut into squares. I make them small.

16 small brownies

2 lbs. yellow squash

SQUASH MUFFINS

1 C butter

1 C sugar

2 eggs

3 C white flour

1 Tbsp. plus 2 tsp. baking powder

1 tsp. salt

Heat oven to 375°F and butter muffin tins for 24 muffins.

Cut squash into 1-inch slices. Cook in a small amount of water for 15 to 20 minutes until very soft. Drain and mash the squash. it should make 2 cups.

Combine squash, eggs, and butter. Set aside.

Sift remaining ingredients into a bowl. Make a well in the center of the flour mixture and add squash mixture, stirring well.

Bake for 20 minutes.

24 muffins

Celebrating the Life

Of

Mother Mildred Butler
"98"

Saturday, April 28, 2018
Viewing: 11:00 a.m. – 12:00 p.m.
Service: 12:00 p.m.

Promise Land Baptist Church
RR 622
Washington, Virginia

Rev. Forrest Freeman, Officiant
Rev. Herbert Johnson, Eulogy

APPENDIX I

Poems
by
Mildred Freeman Butler

LORD TEACH ME TO DO SOME GOOD

While walking along this road of life

If a little child I should meet,

Let me him with a smile greet.

He may need a helping hand

To guide him along this barren land.

Teach me to do some good.

Then as further on I go,

If an adolescent I happen to see,

Let me speak a kind word

For she may also need to be told

How the Saviour can save her soul.

Teach me to do some good.

After I have gone a few miles more

And meet and older person

When his steps are getting very slow,

Let me just stop and see

If of help I may to him be.

Teach me to do some good.

Then when my life can be no more

And I am nearing the eternal shore,

Let me look back and praise the Dear Lord

For teaching me to have done some good.

PRECIOUS MEMORIES

When I was a child, on Granddad's small farm
In the hills of the Blue Ridge Mountains,
We carried water from creeks and springs,
Because there wasn't any plumbing or fountains.

There were gardens, cornfields, apples and other fruit.
We had plenty to eat.
Oh yes! chickens, other fowls and pigs
were raised for meat.

The cows were milked to have cream and butter,
which made our food taste much better.

And a horse named Bill
was hitched to a slide to pull wood from the highest hill.

Granddad had a buggy, and he and grandma rode to church,

store, and a nearby town.

We walked to church, school and houses

in our community close around.

The house was made of logs, but we didn't mind.

With us everything was just fine.

It still stands in the same place,

But has been remodeled and has a new face.

I cherish those memories of long ago,

Even though they can't be any more.

That's why I thank God for that special time,

because it brings much joy and love to my mind.

LITTLE THINGS MEAN A LOT

It isn't the largest things in life, nor the greatest amount.
Sometimes the very smallest can be the ones that count.

Think about the widow's mite, which was once a mere penny.
Why worry if you don't have aplenty.

I'd rather take a lesser part than to extort myself
and leave the greater portion to be enjoyed by someone else.

If someone do me a favor, be it great or small their part,
I'm truly thankful from the bottom of my heart.

Mildred Butler
December 19, 2011

APPENDIX II

History of the
George Washington Carver School
by Lillian Freeman Aylor

Prior to 1948 young Black men and women in Culpeper, Greene, Madison, Orange, and Rappahannock counties experienced extreme difficulties in acquiring a high school Education. Culpeper and Orange counties had a secondary program; however, the offerings were so very limited that some parents paid for their children's attendance to school elsewhere to ensure that they would be admitted to colleges.

Greene, Madison, and Rappahannock counties did not provide an educational opportunity beyond the 7th grade. The children of these counties were forced to gain a high school education elsewhere at the total expense of their parents. Some parents in Rappahannock County sent their children to boarding schools in Manassas and Christiansburg, Virginia.

As a result of the struggle by Black citizens to acquire an equal education for Black children, in 1946 Culpeper and Rappahannock counties signed an agreement that Culpeper would accept the Rappahannock students on a tuition basis. The Rappahannock county students were bussed to Culpeper beginning in the 1946/1947 school year.

However, the continued struggle of the Black citizens in these five counties and the threat of a legal suit caused the governing bodies of Culpeper, Greene, Orange, Madison, and Rappahannock counties to explore the possibility of a regional high school. Later Greene County withdrew and decided to join Albemarle County. The four remaining counties concluded that a regional high school would fulfill the requirement and provide significant economic advantages to the counties. In 1946 the representatives of Orange County proposed to the regional group (Culpeper, Madison, and Rappahannock) a resolution to request the approval and allocation of funds from the Governor of Virginia (Gov. William C. Tuck) to build a regional high school for the Black citizens of these counties. The resolution thus read:

> WHEREAS the counties of Madison and Rappahannock have no high school facilities for Negroes, the county of Orange has but one four-room high school for Negroes, housing at present 125 Negro pupils, and the high school facilities for Negroes at Culpeper are inadequate.
>
> THEREFORE BE IT RESOLVED that the Regional Board of Control of said high school, assembled at Culpeper, Virginia on October 11, 1946, does hereby urge the Honorable William M. Tuck, Governor of the Commonwealth of Virginia, to approve the allocation of $75,000.00 to this project as soon as possible so the said Regional Board of Control may proceed with its plans to erect the high school building for the Negro pupils of the four counties at the earliest possible date.
>
> George Washington Carver Regional High School was named for one of America's greatest scientists, a Black who revolutionized agriculture and economically saved agriculture in the South. It opened its doors October 1, 1948 to 452 students, fourteen teachers, a principal, a secretary, a cafeteria manager, a janitor and many volunteer parent workers. As a result of a rapid increase in enrollment, the school's physical plant was expanded by the addition of eight classrooms and a gymnasium shortly after opening.
>
> George Washington Carver Regional High School quickly gained recognition on the state and national level. It's highly motivated and dedicated students distinguished themselves in high school activities,

in colleges and universities, as citizens and in the workplace.

When George Washington Carver Regional High School closed its doors in 1968, (20 years of service), more that 2500 young Afro-American men and women had graced its classrooms, young men and women who would later make significant contributions to their communities and the Nation. George Washington Carver Regional High School was a special educational institution. It was an educational milestone for Blacks in Culpeper, Madison, Orange and Rappahannock Counties, representing the toil, dedication, commitment, struggle and sacrifice by Black parents to obtain an opportunity for an adequate high school education for their children. It was an institution with a dedicated and committed faculty, who challenged students to their fullest; yet, never failing to encourage those who fell short. Lastly, it was a landmark representing a Black farmer's willingness to give up prime real estate to enhance the educational opportunities of young Black men and women.

APPENDIX III

"Lillian Freeman Aylor—Citizen of the Year"

By Roger Piantadosi
Rappahannock News 28 November 2013

Lillian Freeman Aylor is 75, and not terribly tall, and is quiet and unassuming enough that you could start thinking she's a bit of a wallflower. That would be a mistake. You should have noticed that the reason she isn't doing a lot of talking has to do with the fact that she is doing a lot of doing. And if you're not going to help, by the way, then you best move over closer to that wall yourself.

"She's one of those people who . . . when she says she's there, that she's going to do something, you don't have to second-guess," says her daughter, Kimberly Beard, 49, a Baptist minister who lives in Winchester. "She always comes through. You never have to ask her twice — in fact, most of the time you don't even have to ask her once. She just takes it as a need. And she's that way with her church, her community, her family. She just takes on the role of, 'I'll get it done.'"

"She is a person whose faith in God gets expressed in a willingness to work, and be of service to people," said Barbara Adolfi, a Sperryville therapist and writer. "At her 75th birthday party recently at the Sperryville fire hall, there were at least 100 people there, and so many of them stood up and talked about the many ways in which she cares for other people."

"It is why she treats people the way she does," says Kim Beard, asked about her mother's belief — or her knowing, really — that there is more to life than what most of us see before us on an average day, and thus her strong connection to faith, God, and her church. "She understands that there is more to life.

"We endured a lot of hardships when we were younger, and I'm just going to leave it at that — but her perseverance, her faith, during those struggles, have helped me in so many ways . . . When things don't go the way I might like, I think of my mother. No matter what life throws at her, she kind of plows right through it, with unwavering faith and a positive attitude, that things will get better. And a smile on her face."

The point at which many local folks realize there is more to Aylor than meets the eye is when it instead meets the ear — in other words, when she sings.

"It was at the memorial for Emily Hilscher," says Ray Boc, a longtime Sperryville resident and photographer, speaking of the service held in Rappahannock for the Virginia Tech student who died in the tragic shooting there in 2007. "Lillian got up and sang. She stepped up there and . . . it blew me away, and everyone else. It's a memory I have of her that's really powerful, and it's almost symbolic of what I have learned of Lillian over the years. She's a quiet person; she often looks downward and speaks softly. But when she has something important to say, you listen."

"If I should pre-decease Lillian," says Cliff Miller, whose family has employed Aylor for more than 30 years, "I always say I hope she'll sing at my funeral. It's a special voice. It brings tears to my eyes every time I hear her sing.

"She is one of the most giving people I know," says Miller. "She's a tremendous asset to this community."

Before she would rise to become among the most well-known of those in Rappahannock County's comparatively tiny African-American population, Aylor grew up in Gid Brown Hollow; a studious young woman who became salutatorian of her seventh-grade class in 1952 at the Washington Graded School, the two-room school for black students that once stood on Piedmont Avenue.

Over the years, she taught herself what she needed to know, including cooking and bookkeeping — two skills that served her well when she first went to work for J. Clifford Miller II and his family at Mount Vernon Farm. She now works as co-innkeeper for Miller III, at what is now the Inn at Mount Vernon Farm.

"Yes, she is a person who makes connections, and makes

friends," says her daughter Kim in response to a question. "At the inn, I actually helped her out there over the last couple of months, and all of the comments I heard from guests that stayed there, especially ones that had returned, when they found out I was her daughter, they all said she is one of the reasons why they keep coming back. She is just genuinely warm and friendly, and open to anyone and everyone."

Aylor is secretary of the Rappahannock Convalescent Loan Closet, and has been a Sperryville-Piedmont electoral official for more than 30 years. She's captain of the "Spiritual Walkers" Relay for Life team, treasurer of the Rappahannock Historical Society and vice president of the Scrabble School Preservation Foundation.

She's served on fundraising and steering committees and as a mentor for the Headwaters Foundation, has raised money door-to-door for the American Red Cross and volunteered with the Rappahannock unit of the American Heart Association, serving as its president and vice president; she has also been a vice chair of the Rappahannock Democratic Committee.

At her church, Promise Land Baptist in Gid Brown, she's been vice chair of the deaconess board, president of the senior choir, corresponding secretary, president of the usher's auxiliary, church clerk, chair of the Annual Women's Day and assistant pianist. She's also been pianist at First Baptist Church in Washington for 10 years.

Her piano playing reveals a typical instance of Aylor determination. "Someone needed a pianist, and I think Lillian wanted to learn to play the piano," says Miller. "So when she was 65 or 70, she began taking piano lessons. And she learned."

In 1986, Aylor organized an appreciation for her former seventh-grade teacher, Julia E. Boddie, at the Washington Graded School. With Dorothy Butler, also a former Graded School teacher, they set up a scholarship in Boddie's name, presenting the first award to a RCHS graduate in 1988. The program has grown to be a part of the annual Martin Luther King Jr. celebration every January at the Theatre at Washington, which Theatre owner Wendy Weinberg helped set up. The King program, which includes

"Dream Keeper" awards and an essay contest, will be 23 years old this coming January.

"Lillian has given her time and talents to serving others," says Nan Butler-Roberts, Dorothy Butler's daughter, who now works with Aylor on the Boddie scholarship program. "And she does it very quietly. It's not for show."

For close to 15 years, in addition to her church and community activities, Aylor looked after both her mother and her aunt, who had come to live with her in Sperryville. Both lived into their 90s, and during the years when their health was deteriorating, daughter Kim Beard says, "she managed to take care of them both, and still get everything else done.

These days, Beard says, "mom is like a rock for my sister," referring to her sister Janice Page, who is battling cancer in Charlestown, W.Va. (where a third sibling, William Louis "Pete" Aylor Jr. also lives).

"Mom has been on the forefront of raising money for her," she says. "At her birthday party in October, in fact, instead of asking for gifts,

she wanted everyone to make a donation to help my sister."

Asked how her mother might respond to her choice as a Rappahannock News Citizen of the Year, Kim Beard laughs. "She will probably say, 'Oh, they shouldn't have.'"

Well, they did.

Lillian's 5-Generation Family Tree

(Excluding her paternal grandfather's lines which will appear in a separate chart.)

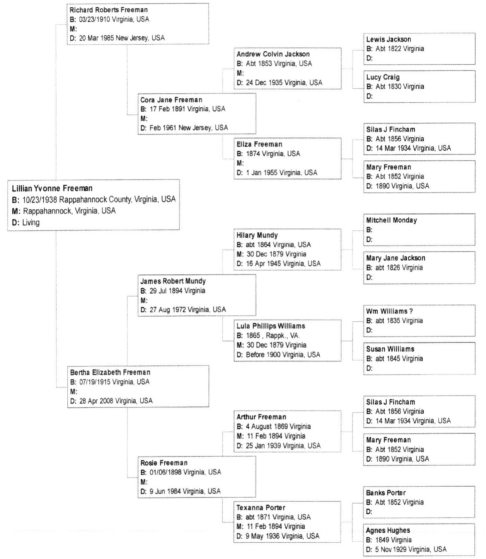

Extended Ancestry finds not shown on this family tree:

Lewis Jackson born approximately 1822 was the son of Rueben and Lety Jackson.

Mary Freeman (1852-1890) was the daughter of Franklin Freeman born around 1820 and Tabitha Freeman.

Banks Porter born around 1852 was the son of Prince Porter and Harriet Porter.

Aggy Hughes born (1849 - 5 November 1829), was the daughter of Charles Hughes and Phoebe Hughes who was born around 1810.

APPENDIX IV

Untangling the Mystery of Lillian Through Genealogy

by Jan McKinney

Who am I? This question contains only three words and six letters, seemingly simple, but for some this simple question can take a lifetime to answer. The answer to this question involves a complex collection of information and experiences. This includes philosophy, spiritual beliefs, demographics, education, career, ancestry and many other facets of what makes us who we are. It was the desire to answer this question that led Lillian to record her memoir. I have had the honor and privilege of assisting her with identifying her ancestors, which will add a small part to her answer to the question of "Who am I?"

Anyone who has ever done family history research knows that things are rarely what we first thought they would be. Our ancestors sometimes hide from us in piles of ancient documents. Sometimes the identity of an ancestor may offer great surprise. When Lillian and Barbara first asked me to help with this project the official scope of my work was to simply type up a family tree and to hopefully fill in some missing pieces through DNA results. A simple task, right? Well that was over a year ago and during that time, Lillian and I have been on a research roller coaster! We have found many amazing discoveries, including the fact that Lillian and I are cousins! As with all genealogical research there have been shocks, surprises and even some humor. The running joke with "Team Lillian" (as we call ourselves) is that between my "kin folk," her "kin folk" and our shared "kin" we probably are related to 75% of the native population of Rappahannock County!

In this section you will find descendants charts and ancestry family tree pedigree charts. Lillian has been given copies of supporting documents including: photographs, birth certificates, death certificates, marriage licenses, census records and military records. There is a section on the procedure and results in locating information on the identity of Lillian's paternal great-grandfather. There is a collection of general histories on various connected surnames and some narrative explanation regarding DNA results.

The Grandfather Mystery

The identity of Lillian's biological paternal great-grandfather has been uncertain since his birth in the early 20th century. At the time DNA testing for paternity did not exist. Oral tradition was that his identity was that of a Miller neighbor. This was presumed true by Lillian and her family members. However, when we started working on Lillian's DNA matches we found that this could not be the case as she was not related to any close descendants of the Miller family who had taken DNA tests that were published on Ancestry.com. After months of contacting other matches, comparing trees and ethnicity results, I was able to narrow down the matches of her paternal grandfather's line. Then based on census and other contemporary records from the time period of 1908-1910 was able to determine who had reasonable proximity. Next I was able to narrow down the prospects to two possibilities, who were first cousins. Once these two possibilities were identified, descendants' charts were built and potential DNA matches sought.

Based on this information the most probable identity of her biological paternal great-grandfather would be Harry Jackson Monroe. Harry's family had resided in Gid Brown Hollow since the beginning of Rappahannock County. He had Monroes on his father's side and the Houghtons on his mother's side. (His family tree is on page 136.)

During the late 19th century many of the family branches began to move west, to Ohio, Kansas and Missouri. Harry was born in Kansas, but his family had returned to Gid Brown Hollow. Sometime after 1900 his parents and siblings moved back west, this time to Ohio, but he remained with his maternal aunts, Ann and Mary Houghton who lived in Gid Brown Hollow (Census Dwelling no. 183 in Hampton District). Harry was approximately 21 at the time of the 1910 census.

Lillian's paternal great-grandmother, Jane (Cora Jane) Freeman was living with her mother Lizzy and her siblings in Gid Brown Hollow at the time of the 1910 Census (Census Dwelling no. 168 Hampton District). She was approximately 19 years old at the time of the census. Richard Roberts Freeman was born 23 March 1910.

At the time of the 1910 Census Lillian's alleged great-grandfather, Harry Monroe had been unemployed for 3 months. Sometime between the census taking and June 1917 he moved west to Iowa, likely for work. Based on records found for him, he remained in the mid-west, living in Iowa, Nebraska and finally dying in Arkansas in 1969. No evidence was found that he married or had other children.

The identification of Harry Jackson Monroe as the biological father of Richard Roberts Freeman is not 100% certain. It is a statistical probability based on available DNA evidence and proximity according to Census and other records. Without further DNA evidence, which is not available at this time and may not ever be available, we cannot state with 100% certainty that Harry J. Monroe was the father of Lillian's grandfather but can state that there is a strong likelihood. We can, however, state that the oral history of a Miller neighbor as the father is 100% not accurate based on DNA analysis.

Native American Ancestry

Part of Lillian's story involves oral history about Native American ancestry on Rosie Freeman's line (maternal grandmother). Both Ancestry.com and 23andme.com tests show that Lillian does have approximately .5%-1% Native American ethnicity. Statistically this would mean that her "full-blooded" Native American ancestor could be found around 7 generations removed from Lillian.[1] Based on research by Craig Smedley, one of Lillian's cousins found through Ancestry.com DNA matching, he also has Native ancestry and he and Lillian share a connection through Tabitha Freeman. This was Lillian's maternal and paternal 3rd great-grandmother who was born in the early 1800s. Given these scenarios the Native ancestor could be one of Tabitha Freeman's parents or grandparents. To date, the evidence shows this only as a possibility.

Franklin Freeman (c. 1820) and Tabitha Freeman were the parents of Mary Freeman (c.1852-c.1890). [See the 5-Generation family tree on page 122.]

Fincham Family

Lillian is descended from the Fincham family on both her maternal and paternal lines. Her family tree shows lineage to five generations ending with Silas Fincham. I have researched this line back an additional two generations to include Harrison Fincham (1829-1902) and Celia Catherine Leake Fincham (1825-1910), daughter of Elias Leake, as parents of Silas Fincham. The last generation proved so far is that of William Fincham (b.1773-1833) and Elizabeth McAlister Fincham (b. 1790) as parents of Harrison Fincham.

This line stems through the relationship between Silas Fincham and Mary Freeman, Lillian's great-grandmother. Silas Fincham was Caucasian and Mary Freeman is listed as "mulatto" or "black." Together they had a number of children, but their marriage would have been illegal at the time.

Therefore, there was no written documentation of Silas Fincham being the father of Mary Freeman's children. This research began with oral history. However, Lillian has over 300 DNA matches with Fincham relatives, some as close as second cousins. The relationships shown through these matches align with the relationship stated in Lillian's oral history. This is where Lillian and I share a cousinship. My common ancestor with Lillian would be a Fincham from the mid-18th century.

The Fincham family originated in southern England and there is still a town called Fincham, England, located in Norfolk. The name Fincham appears to pre-date the Norman invasion of 1066 as a derivative of "Fincham" is said to appear in a document during the time of Edward the Confessor.[2]

The Finchams of this area likely are the descendants of two brothers who were transported from Essex, England, to Virginia on a ship called The Essex in 1740. According to Essex Assize Court records from 1739 John and Robert Fincham were found guilty of "felonies" (unspecified) and transported in lieu of prison time. It is unclear what "crime" they committed.[3] It is possible it was a traditional crime such as theft but given the time period there is a strong possibility that their crime could have been either political or religious in nature. From the time of the English Civil War to the Revolutionary War many thousands of people were transported as rebels from the Britain to America. Peter Wilson Coldham's compilations of bonded and transported passengers are wonderful resources for this type of "immigration." John and Robert Fincham are listed in his books.[4]

John appears to have moved to the Culpeper, Virginia area and Robert went to North Carolina. John Fincham is the likely grandfather of William Fincham who is Lillian's ancestor. Research continues to identify the link between William Fincham, Lillian's ancestor and John Fincham transported from England in 1740.

Concluding Thoughts

The journey of uncovering the mysteries of the past, like life, can be frustrating and exhilarating all at the same time. There are confirmations and surprises. In the end, learning more about our ancestors and their unique stories can be a valuable tool in understanding more about the answer to the question of "Who am I."

It has been a true honor to walk with Lillian on her journey of ancestral discovery.

DNA Results and Genealogy Research

Ancestry.com DNA Results. October 2019.[5]

DNA Results Summary for Lillian Yvonne Freeman Aylor

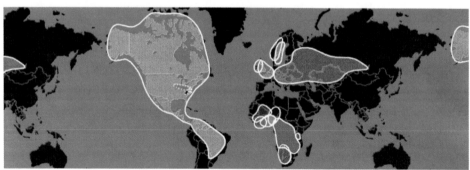

© Mapbox, © OpenStreetMa

Ethnicity Estimate

England, Wales & Northwestern Europe	36%
Benin/Togo	16%
Cameroon, Congo, & Southern Bantu Peoples	13%
Ivory Coast/Ghana	12%
Mali	9%
Norway	4%
Nigeria	4%
Ireland & Scotland	2%
Africa South-Central Hunter-Gatherers	1%
Sweden	1%
Native American—North, Central, South	1%
Eastern Europe & Russia	1%

Additional Communities

Early Virginia African Americans

The Carolinas, Maryland & Virginia African Americans

Northern Virginia African Americans

Ohio River Valley, Indiana, Illinois & Iowa Settlers

Figure 1

23andMe DNA Results. October 2019.[6]

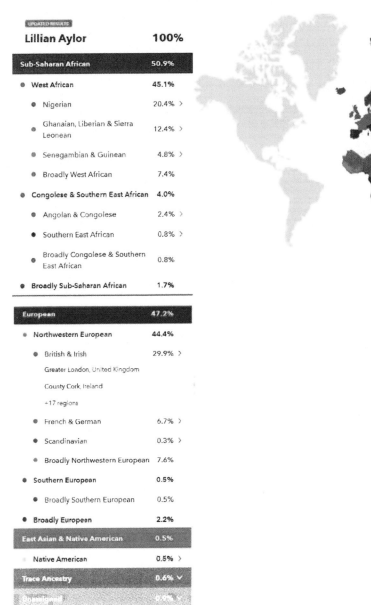

Descendant Charts

The following Descendant's Charts are presented in a slightly modified NGSQ "system". (National Genealogical Society Quarterly System is a recognized procedural standard for published Genealogical Charts)

NOTE:
Lillian's ancestry is a work in progress. The family tree on page 122 comprises information on four generations past Lillian, with several lines going back five and six generations. The chart is comprised of information gained through standard records such as birth, marriage, and death certificates, wills, census, and military records. There were areas of her tree where we had to begin with oral history alone, as that was all that had been available for generations. DNA testing now helps with identifying mystifying ancestors who are not readily available on paper.

Lillian took two DNA tests, the first through 23andMe and the second through Ancestry.com. Wherever we began with just oral history, we sought to clarify and prove lines through DNA matches supplemented by corresponding records. Through this tedious process we were able to shed some light in areas that had not previously been known or provable.

Lillian's Paternal Line

Generation 1

1. **Cora Jane Freeman,** daughter of **Andrew Colvin Jackson** and **Eliza Freeman** was born on 17 February 1891 in Rappahannock County Virginia, United States, and died in New Jersey, United States, February 1961.

Cora Jane Freeman had a relationship with an unknown father, who appears from DNA matches to possibly be Harry Jackson Monroe, who was the son of Silas M. Monroe and Edwina Houghton Monroe, and was born 22 August 1888 in Concordia, Kansas, United States and who died 3 October 1969 in Pope County Arkansas, United States. He resided in Gid Brown Hollow (Hampton District), Washington, Virginia, United States from at least 1900 to 1910. He appears to have never married.

Child of this relationship:

+ 2. M i. **Richard Roberts Freeman** was born 23 March 1910, Rappahannock County, Virginia, United States and died 20 March 1985 in Plainfield, Union, New Jersey, United States.

Generation 2 (modified formatting)

2. **Richard Roberts Freeman** had a common law relationship with Bertha Elizabeth Freeman.

Children of this relationship:

+ 3. F i. **Lillian Yvonne Freeman** was born 23 October 1938, Rappahannock County, Virginia, United States

4. M ii. **James Robert Freeman** was born 24 March 1941, Rappahannock County, Virginia, United States. He married Charlotte Barbour and had the following children: James Robert Freeman, Jr. and Dexter Brown Freeman.

5. M iii. **Forrest Lee Freeman** was born 31 October 1943, Rappahannock County, Virginia, United States. With Jacqueline Porter he had: Cristol Porter, Jeffrey Porter and Anthony Porter. He married Nancy Jones and had the following children: Forrest Lee Freeman, Jr. and Marsha Freeman.

Richard Roberts Freeman married Estelle Erwin (1909-2009) on 1 March 1947 in Manhattan, New York City, New York, United States.

Children of this relationship:

6. F. i. **Barbara Freeman** was born 9 May 1947, in New Jersey, United States. She married Alfred Hemmons and they had Katrina and Robin.

7. M ii. **Richard Freeman** was born 13 January 1949, in New Jersey, United States. He married Leigh and they had Jessica.

8. M. iii. **William Freeman** was born 6 May 1952 in New Jersey, United States. He married (1) Gwedolyn and they had Keri and Ashley. He married (2) Ellen, no children were born of this relationship.

Generations 3-5 (modified formatting)

3. **Lillian Yvonne Freeman** married William Lewis Aylor on
   23 June 1957 in Rappahannock County, Virginia, United States.

Children of this relationship:

> 9. M i. **William Lewis Aylor, Jr.** was born
>   25 May 1958, Front Royal, Warren County,
>   Virginia, United States and married (1)
>   Tracey Veeney and they had Natasha Aylor.
>   He married (2) Priscilla Vigay and they had
>   William Joseph Aylor.
>
> 10. F ii. **Janice Lee Aylor,** was born
>   3 January 1961, Front Royal, Warren County,
>   Virginia United States and married
>   (1) Haywood Turner. They had **Christopher
>   Tremaine Turner.** She married (2) Calvin
>   Page. She died 27 August 2015 in Ranson,
>   West Virginia, United States.
>
>> **Christopher Tremaine Turner** married
>> Keosha and they had Chloe, Tremaine
>> and Cecilia.
>
> 11. F iii. **Kimberly Anne Aylor** was born
>   9 August 1964, Front Royal, Warren County,
>   Virginia, United States. She married Jeff
>   Beard and they had **Landrum Beard** and
>   **Taylor Yvonne Beard.**

Lillian's Maternal Line

Generation 1

1. **Rosie Freeman,** daughter of Arthur Freeman and Texanna Porter Freeman, was born 6 January 1898, Rappahannock County, Virginia, United States. She died 9 June 1984, Washington, Rappahannock County, Virginia United States. Rosie Freeman had a common law relationship with James Robert Mundy.

Children of this relationship:

+   2.   F.   i.   **Bertha Elizabeth Freeman**, was born 19 July 1915, Rappahannock County, Virginia, United States. She died 28 April 2008, Culpeper County, Virginia, United States.

      3.   F.   ii.   **Margaret Allbright Freeman**, was born 12 December 1917, Rappahannock County, Virginia, United States. She married Haywood Poles. She died 7 March 2012.

Generation 2

2. **Bertha Elizabeth Freeman** had a common law relationship with Richard Roberts Freeman.

Children of this relationship:

      4.   F   i.   **Lillian Yvonne Freeman** was born 23 October 1938, Rappahannock County, Virginia, United States. [See paternal chart for progeny.]

      5.   M   ii.   **James Robert Freeman** was born 24 March 1941, Rappahannock County, Virginia, United States. [See paternal chart for progeny.]

      6.   M   iii.   **Forrest Lee Freeman** was born 31 October 1943, Rappahannock County, Virginia, United States. [See paternal chart for progeny]

Bertha Elizabeth Freeman had a common law relationship with Raymond Poles.

Children of this relationship:

7. F. iv. **Anna Rose Freeman** was born 30 May 1947, Rappahannock County, Virginia, United States. She married (1) Wallace Carter – no progeny and (2) Wash Morton and they had the following children: Brenda Renee Morton, Ramona Inez Morton, Stephanie Fay Morton, Wash Morton, Jr., and Elizabeth Pearl Morton.

8. F. v. **Darlene Elizabeth Freeman** was born 14 April 1953, Warren County, Virginia, United States. She married (1) Wardell Russell and they had Wardell Russell, Jr. and

   (2) John Ferguson and they had Lakisha Ferguson.

9. F. vi. **Arlene Bernice Freeman** was born 14 April 1953, Warren County, Virginia, United States. She married (1) Edward Bailey, Jr. – no progeny and (2) Charles Green and they had Charles Green, Jr. and Tracey Lynn Green.

Line of Harry Jackson Monroe

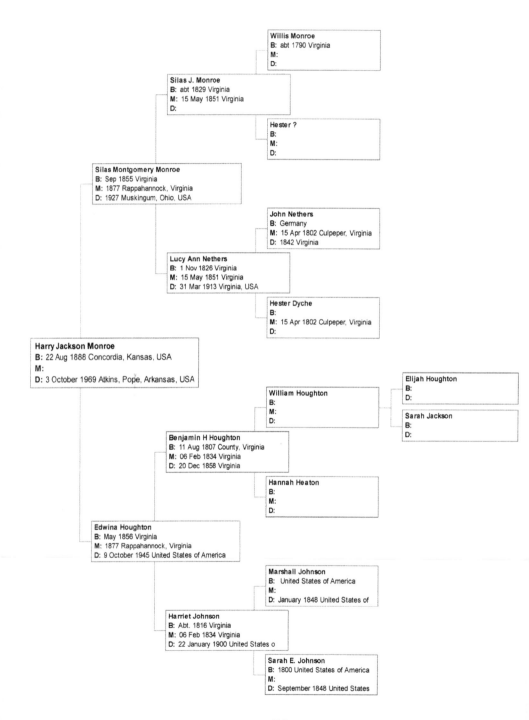

Willis Monroe
B: abt 1790 Virginia
M:
D:

Silas J. Monroe
B: abt 1829 Virginia
M: 15 May 1851 Virginia
D:

Hester ?
B:
M:
D:

Silas Montgomery Monroe
B: Sep 1855 Virginia
M: 1877 Rappahannock, Virginia
D: 1927 Muskingum, Ohio, USA

John Nethers
B: Germany
M: 15 Apr 1802 Culpeper, Virginia
D: 1842 Virginia

Lucy Ann Nethers
B: 1 Nov 1826 Virginia
M: 15 May 1851 Virginia
D: 31 Mar 1913 Virginia, USA

Hester Dyche
B:
M: 15 Apr 1802 Culpeper, Virginia
D:

Harry Jackson Monroe
B: 22 Aug 1888 Concordia, Kansas, USA
M:
D: 3 October 1969 Atkins, Pope, Arkansas, USA

Elijah Houghton
B:
D:

William Houghton
B:
M:
D:

Sarah Jackson
B:
D:

Benjamin H Houghton
B: 11 Aug 1807 County, Virginia
M: 06 Feb 1834 Virginia
D: 20 Dec 1858 Virginia

Hannah Heaton
B:
M:
D:

Edwina Houghton
B: May 1856 Virginia
M: 1877 Rappahannock, Virginia
D: 9 October 1945 United States of America

Marshall Johnson
B: United States of America
M:
D: January 1848 United States of

Harriet Johnson
B: Abt. 1816 Virginia
M: 06 Feb 1834 Virginia
D: 22 January 1900 United States o

Sarah E. Johnson
B: 1800 United States of America
M:
D: September 1848 United States

Endnotes:

1 Morcillo, Patrick (PhD Genetics and Herdity Cornell University). n.d. Quora. Accessed October 6, 2019. https://www.quora.com/If-you-have-1-of-an-area-in-your-DNA-how-many-generations-back-would-that-be. To determine possible connections with this small amount of DNA I followed the formula according to Patrick Morcillo, Ph D Genetics and Heredity, Cornell University, "assuming that all your ancestors are not related, just solve the formula: $0.5^n=0.01$. Or $2^n=100$. 2,4,8,16,32,64,128 =6–7 generations."

2 2019. Finchams. Accessed October 6, 2019. http://www.finchams.org/.

3 Fincham, Sherry Sorrells. 2016. Roots Web. Accessed October 6, 2019. https://wc.rootsweb.com/cgi-bin/igm.cgi?db=finchum&id=I399&op=GET.

4 The Complete Book of Emigrants 1700-1750, By Peter Wilson Coldham.

5 Ancestry.com DNA Ethnicity Estimates valid as of 30 September 2019 – reprinted with the acknowledgement of Ancestry.com

6 DNA Ethnicity Estimates valid as of 7 October 2019 from 23andme.com – reprinted with acknowledgement of 23andme.com

Lillian Freeman Aylor

Lillian Freeman Aylor, born in 1938 in a log cabin in the foothills of the Blue Ridge Mountains of Virginia, has been a quiet but steady force for change over a lifetime in Rappahannock County, Virginia. An election official for thirty years, and an officer in the local Democratic Committee, she worked to protect voting rights. For many years she has been on the Board of the Scrabble School Preservation Foundation which houses the African-American Heritage Center in a restored Rosenwald School. She was the first African-American on the board of the Rappahannock Historical Society, a deaconess in the Promised Land Baptist Church, and a founding member of the Unity Choir. She has a been central to supporting the county's faith community a continuous supporter of African-American choral music.

At a time when school for African-American children ended in 7th grade, Lillian attended the Washington (Virginia) Graded School then took the bus to Culpeper to graduate fourth in her class from George Washington Carver Regional High School. Married at eighteen to local horse trainer Moody Aylor, she had three children—Pete, Janice and Kim. After a divorce in 1978, Lillian enrolled in a computer training program in Springfield, VA., worked as a proof operator in a bank, then returned to her rural home county to become the bookkeeper and housekeeper for the Mount. Vernon Stock Farm. In 2011 she became the innkeeper and chef for the renovated, historic Inn at Mount Vernon Farm where her cooking has become renown.

At 81, Lillian continues to live independently and is an officer in many community and church organizations . "She always comes through," says her daughter Kim. "You never have to ask her twice."

Made in the USA
Middletown, DE
28 October 2021